Henry George Willink

A Biography of

H. G. Willink

1851 – 1938

by
Malcolm Summers

About the author:

Malcolm Summers worked at The Willink School from 1988 to 2017, as Head of Maths, then Assistant Deputy Head, and as Deputy Head from 1993. Originally from Birmingham, he has lived in Reading for over 35 years. He is married with two grown up children.

Malcolm Summers has also written:
History of Greyfriars Church, Reading – available from Greyfriars Bookshop, Reading, and other local bookshops.

Nicolas Appert (who invented the process of preserving food used in canning) – available from Amazon.

Published by Downs Way Publishing
1 Downs Way, Tilehurst, Reading RG31 6SL

ISBN 978-0-9927515-3-1

The initial letter illustrations at the beginning of each chapter are by Henry George Willink.

Front cover: Henry George Willink (aged 61), by his sister-in-law Harriet Delamain Clark in 1912.
(By kind permission of the The Willink School)

Dedication:

To my wife
Cathy

Fides et Amor

The biographer's dilemma...

It is always a difficult decision: how should the author refer to the subject of a biography? Often the subject's surname is chosen, and certainly in shorter or formal works this would be standard. Perhaps it is my long association with The Willink School, known locally as just "Willink," that made me feel that I wanted to identify more closely with the person of Henry George, and so the use of his surname did not appeal.

In his writings and, for example, his photograph album annotations, he called himself – and others – by initials, and so "HGW" is a strong contender. My first draft, in fact, used HGW throughout. On reflection, however, it did not make the text flow as I wished it to. In discussion with members of the Willink family, we decided that it would be in keeping with Henry's own usage if I were to use HGW on annotations for sketches and photographs.

For repeated use in the text, "Henry George" (and the middle name was important to him) seemed too cumbersome. What other possibilities were there? His father, rather obscurely, always called him Dicky. His grandchildren's generation called him (as we shall see) Ba – pronounced "Bar." Those not in the family would have called him Mr. Willink. The local press and official documents named him formally as Mr. H. G. Willink. None of these would do.

I imagine, however, that his peers, particularly his wife and close friends, would have known him simply as "Henry." And so, at risk of seeming too informal, I decided that I too would call him Henry.

Chapter		Page
	Fides et Amor – Faith & Love	ix
1	The Willink Family	1
2	School and University Days	15
3	Life in London	29
4	Highwoods	61
5	Guardian of the Poor	81
6	Hillfields	89
7	A Berkshire Alderman	107
8	The War Years	121
9	Twilight	141
	Epilogue - Hillfields	157
	Acknowledgements	159
	Endnotes & Sources	161
	List of Illustrations	187
	Index	191

Fides et Amor – Faith & Love

A glass I

t was at the fifth meeting of the Governing Body of the yet-to-be-opened Burghfield Secondary Modern School on 11 October 1956, that the newly elected Vice Chairman, Major L. M. E. Dent D.S.O., suggested that the school should be named The Willink School in recognition of the late Mr. H. G. Willink.[1]

Among various aspects of Mr. Willink's service to the community, Major Dent mentioned that he had been an Alderman of Berkshire County Council and Chairman of the Education Committee, a resident of Burghfield and a leading man in the local community. It was agreed to write to Mr. F. A. Willink, Henry Willink's son and now the head of the family, for official approval of the proposal.

The school itself had a connection to Mr. H. G. Willink since it had been built on land that was part of the Hillfields estate that he had owned. The land had been purchased by Berkshire County Council from Major Dent, who was himself a relative by marriage of the Willink family.[2]

Approval of the proposal having been given by the family, The Willink School opened on Tuesday 8 January 1957, with 114 girls and 131 boys on roll organised into 9 classes, with Mr. Noel Jackson as Headmaster and 11 assistant teaching staff. Later that month, Governors agreed that the school uniform should be navy blue and that the school badge should be based on the Willink coat of arms. By further agreement with the Willink family, their motto – *Fides et Amor* – also became the school motto. A large Willink shield hung on the back wall of the school hall for many years; now each student wears the design on their uniform.

Henry George Willink had died in 1938, almost 20 years earlier. He was a man of many talents and interests, who made contributions to both local and national society. He was a barrister, mountaineer, fencer, artist and illustrator, and noted speaker. He was also, and pre-eminently, a family man.

The school keeps his name alive. I hope that this book will do the same for his story.

HGW
Henry George Willink

Aged 50, in 1901

HGW's father,
William Williamson Willink

Painted by Lance Calkin (1859 – 1936) [3]

Chapter 1

The Willink Family

A chamber scene

enry George Willink was born in the afternoon of Thursday 10 July 1851 at his parents' house in Belvedere Road, Princes Park, Liverpool.[4] Henry was the third child of the impressively named William Williamson Willink and his wife Catharine.

Within forty-eight hours, baby Henry was fighting for his life in the grip of scarlet fever. The family's older son had been the first to contract the fever several months before, followed soon after by William. Both bouts had been mild and they had made a full recovery. No-one else, Catharine or any of their three servants, had developed any symptoms. This lulled the family into a false sense of security, compounded by advice from a distinguished London surgeon, Mr. Hodgson, who reassured the expectant mother that, in view of her condition, she was not liable to come down with the disease.

However, Catharine did develop scarlet fever soon after Henry, and despite all efforts she died five days after Henry's birth. She was just 26 years old. On Tuesday 22 July, Catharine was buried in the churchyard of St. Michael's Church in Huyton, beside her infant daughter Harriet who had died five years earlier.[5]

HGW's mother,
Catharine Harriet Willink (née Nicholls)

Painted by Thomas Richmond (1802 – 1874)
soon after her marriage in 1844

William was back in church on the next day for his baby son's baptism at St. John the Baptist, Princes Park.[6] Henry fully recovered from his bout of scarlet fever, but he retained something of a sickly nature for much of his childhood.

The surname Willink is sufficiently unusual for its origin in England to be traceable. There was only one Willink family in the whole of the country in the 1841 census. This was the household of Henry's grandparents, Daniel and Anne.[7] It was this Daniel who brought the surname to England from his native Netherlands.

Referring to the acorns that are in the family arms, Henry wrote the following verse to accompany his family tree:

By Grace of God our Willink oak doth stand
Sprung from Dutch Acorn set in English Land,
Long may the branches of so fair a Tree
Of such seed, and soil, right worthy be.[8]

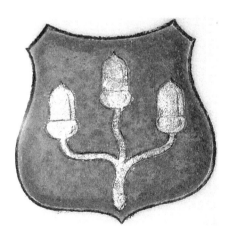

The Willink Shield

From Captain
G. O. W. Willink's
memorial tablet
in St. Mary's Church,
Burghfield

The Willink Family Grant of Arms was only awarded in England in 1931 when Henry and his cousin Alfred Henry

3

Willink (at that time High Sheriff of Westmoreland) acceded to an invitation from the College of Arms to register the old Willink armorial bearings (at a cost, which they shared). All descendants of Daniel Willink are entitled to bear the Willink Arms. The shield is blue with three golden acorns on a sprig, and at the base of the crest "a right arm couped at the elbow and inclined, bearing a wreath, all proper." [9]

Henry halved the Willink shield with his wife's Ouvry family shield, to give the armorial "achievement" below.

The Willink/Ouvry
Shield
Motto: Fides et Amor
(Faith and Love)

From
Henry George Willink's
memorial tablet
in St. Mary's Church,
Burghfield

It is this Willink/Ouvry shield that The Willink School now uses (having used the Three Acorns version on page 3 until the 1970s), including the Willink family motto:

The
Willink School
Shield

4

Henry's father, William Williamson Willink, was the first of the family to be born in England. William's father, Daniel, had been born in Amsterdam in 1779 into a family of successful merchants and bankers.[10] Daniel moved to England in 1804 to take charge of his father's business interests here.

In March 1808 Daniel married Anne Latham.[11] They settled initially in London and it was there that their first child was born on 9 December 1808 at Champion Hill, Camberwell. The child's intended baptismal names were Wilhem Williamson Willink, naming him after his two godfathers – his grandfather Wilhem and a Mr. Joseph Williamson, a friend of Daniel's. However, it was later discovered that his first name had been incorrectly entered into the parish register as William. Daniel and Anne decided that this should become his name in accordance with the legal register.[12]

The family moved to Richmond, Surrey, about 1810 and then to Great George Square in Liverpool in 1813.[13] Daniel was appointed the Consul for the Kingdom of the Netherlands in Liverpool in January 1814, a role he maintained until his death.[14]

Daniel formed a merchant partnership with his brother Jan Abraham and his brother-in-law Charles Latham. Jan Abraham was the agent for the firm in the United States, but his business deals there were marred by an "extravagant and speculative disposition... his transactions and drafts to an immense extent never accounted for." [15] These speculations led directly to the ruin of the firm in 1819, turning an annual profit of approximately £10,000 to a staggering loss of £130,000, and so bankruptcy.

Because of the bankruptcy, the family (by this time Daniel and Anne had 2 boys and 4 girls) [16] had to move to less grand accommodation in Bootle. William, aged 10, was away at school at Ince in Cheshire at the time this happened, but the family uncertainty would nevertheless have affected him deeply.

However, Daniel was irrepressible and he rapidly began to rebuild his fortunes. By 1824 the family were able to live once more in spacious style, moving to 61 Rodney Street, a house with nine bedrooms (not counting those for the servants), and a stable and a coach house behind.[17]

Daniel overreached himself again, resulting in a second bankruptcy in 1829 with debts in the region of £70,000 [18] and so the family had to downsize once more, this time to South Hill Place in Toxteth Park.[19]

The repeated financial difficulties faced by the family meant that William was not able to complete his education by attending university, a lack he felt acutely.[20] His accomplishments were, nevertheless, many – not least in terms of being a talented linguist, fluent in Latin, Greek, French, Dutch, German, Italian and Spanish! [21]

Meanwhile Daniel, with son William now as an employee, decided to start up a new business as a commission merchant. His projects were various: a middle man for passengers wishing to travel by ship; an underwriter of maritime insurance risks; and by 1837, an agent for Palladium Life Assurance Society of London.[22]

In his early twenties, William had a singular experience. In 1829, about £150,000 worth of jewels were stolen from the Princess of Orange at Brussels. Most were recovered at Liverpool two years later. By virtue of his father's role as Consul, William was selected to convey the jewels back to their rightful owner. He travelled with the jewels sewn into his coat, leaving on 10 October and placing them into the Princess's hands 5 days later. As a token of her gratitude, the Princess gave William an amethyst ring set with 64 diamonds. As this was rather large for a ring, William later had it reset as a brooch, which could be converted at will to a pendant.[23]

The Princess of Orange's Jewel

An amethyst set with diamonds,
reset as a brooch/pendant

William stayed with his father's business until 1834, at which time he joined Messrs. Barings in an unpaid position, hoping for a partnership in the firm. Unfortunately, this did not materialise, and so after two years he left, now aged 27 and with few prospects. In the following year, he was asked by Messrs. Fawcett, Preston & Co. of the Phoenix Iron Foundry in Liverpool whether he would go to Leghorn, Italy, on their behalf to use legal processes to recover monies owed to the firm. William negotiated terms with them, which included him becoming a partner of the firm for a period of 15 years. In view of the capital he brought to the firm (£5,000 – much of which was a loan to him by his grandfather Willink) he was to receive one sixth of any profits or losses the firm made annually during that time. It took from April to October 1837 to conclude the Italian business, but William was successful in his mission. On his return journey, he travelled via Holland and applied for the post of Vice Consul for the Netherlands at Liverpool. The appointment was conferred upon him the following year.[24]

The financial rewards of the partnership at the Phoenix Iron Foundry fluctuated greatly over the ensuing years. By 1843, William's share of the profits had totalled £6,500 but then he had to pay out over £7,500 due to losses in the following three years.[25] All in all, his partnership did not lead to financial stability!

In 1839, William's father Daniel purchased a one and a quarter acre plot of land for £1,450 at Barn Hey (sometimes known as Barnhey) on Aigburth Road in Toxteth Park and had a house built there. William, now just into his 30s, was living with his parents still. Daniel retired from commercial life in 1841, upon receipt of a legacy of approximately £25,000 following his father Wilhem's death earlier that year.[26] In early 1842, on the marriage of Princess Sophia of the Netherlands, Daniel was created a Knight of the Order of the Netherland Lion, an award given to those considered to be eminent individuals in their sphere.[27]

On 1 December 1842, William Williamson Willink's life changed. While at a dance in Roby, near Liverpool, he met and fell in love with a charming young lady – Catharine Harriet Nicholls.[28]

Catharine was born on 29 August 1824 at Longford House in Gloucester. She had an itinerant childhood, living in Birmingham, London and Dublin, before settling in London again by the time she was 18. These moves followed her father's public career.

Catharine's father, George Nicholls, was born on the last day of 1781 in Trenithen, Cornwall, of a farming family background.[29] However, George's desire was for the sea, and so aged 15 in March 1797 he sailed as a midshipman on the

Earl of Abergavenny, an East India Company ship, bound for Bombay and China. In subsequent voyages, he served as fifth, third then first mate. He was then given his own ship, the *Lady Lushington*, in 1809 – thus becoming a Captain at age 27. In all he sailed on nine voyages over eighteen years' service.

In 1813 Captain George Nicholls married Harriet Maltby,[30] daughter of Brough and Mary Maltby, at Southwell Cathedral.[31]

In January 1815 George's ship, the *Bengal*, was burned and lost when in harbour at Point de Galle, Ceylon (now Sri Lanka). George was absolved of all blame at the subsequent hearing, but nevertheless he was left with a huge loss of around £80,000 to bear. As a result, he decided to leave the sea.

George and Harriet settled in Farndon, near Newark, and then in Southwell by 1819. At Southwell, George began to be involved in the administration of the Poor Law, becoming a parish overseer of the poor and churchwarden, and establishing the parish as a model of economy. George's main aim was to abolish – or at the least significantly reduce – outdoor relief. As we shall see, Henry followed in his grandfather's footsteps when he was chairman of the Guardians of the Poor at Bradfield Union many years later.

Their next move was to Gloucester, with George becoming the superintendent of the cutting of the Gloucester and Berkeley Canal, working closely with the engineer, Thomas Telford. This started a long-term interest in investment and development of canals, in particular with the Birmingham Canal Navigations Company.

Following the successful opening of the Gloucester and Berkeley Canal, George changed career again, becoming, on 1 January 1827, the manager of the newly opened branch of the Bank of England in Birmingham. The family [32] then lived on the Bank's premises for most of the time they were in Birmingham.

George continued to be in demand for his opinion on Poor Law matters and it came as little surprise to anyone when the Government had passed the Poor Law Amendment Act and was looking for three Commissioners to make the new system work, that George was asked, by letter from Lord Melbourne, the Prime Minister, to become one of the three. Thus was the rest of George's life's work decided. The family left Birmingham for London in mid-September 1834.

Unfortunately, the house they first took in London, at Portman Square, proved to have poor drainage and fever broke out among the family, claiming the lives of two of George and Harriet's daughters in March 1835. George bought two new houses – 16 and 17 Hyde Park Street – and moved into No. 17 as soon as it was finished. At this date, these two houses stood alone in fields.

George and family then spent four years in Ireland from September 1838, where he was entrusted with the implementation of the new Poor Law there. The family moved back to Hyde Park Street in London in December 1842. It was on their journey back from Ireland, briefly stopping over at Liverpool, that William Williamson Willink met George's daughter Catharine at a dance.

The Poor Law Board was reorganised in 1847 and George became its permanent secretary. In 1848 George was honoured by Queen Victoria for his work since 1834, being made a Companion of the Order of the Bath. Following his retirement from the Poor Law Board in January 1851, he was made Knight Commander of the Order of the Bath, thereby becoming Sir George Nicholls, K.C.B. He received his knighthood on 7 August 1851 at Buckingham Palace.[33]

Thus, both of Henry's grandfathers were knights, one of the Order of the Netherland Lion, and the other of the British Order of the Bath.

After a brief engagement, William Williamson Willink married Catharine Harriet Nicholls (aged 19 and so still a minor in the eyes of the law) on 4 June 1844 at St. John the Evangelist's Church, Paddington.[34] The newlyweds honeymooned in Belgium and the Netherlands. On their return, they took up residence in a six-bedroomed rented house in Roby, six miles from Liverpool.[35]

Very sadly, they lost their first child, Harriet Anne, who was born in October 1845 and died aged ten months.[36] Following the birth, Catharine was very unwell, and had to remain in bed for several months.

With their financial situation being unstable due to William's partnership at the Phoenix Iron Foundry, at the end of 1846 William and Catharine had to leave their house at Roby and they moved to live with William's parents at Barn Hey. William Nicholls Willink, their second child (known in the family as Willy) was born there on 10 July 1847, exactly four years before Henry. They stayed at Barn Hey until September 1850, when they moved to a new house on Belvedere Road, Princes Park.[37]

William could afford to move from his parents' house because he had negotiated a change in the terms of his partnership at Phoenix from 1850. Instead of the proportional share of profit or loss, with all its fluctuations, for a binding term of five years he was to be paid £500 per year plus 5% of the profits of the business if any.[38]

It was in this house in Belvedere Road in the following July that Henry George was born, and his mother tragically died. William's mother, Anne ("Grandmamma Willink"), became the two boys' surrogate mother and cared for them throughout the time they stayed in Liverpool. Henry "remembered her well and loved her dearly, and she had particular affection for [Henry]."[39]

William was finally free from his partnership with Phoenix Iron Foundry after 31 December 1854. His family and friends had been on the lookout for a new post for him. His uncle, Alfred Latham, proposed him as the next Secretary to the Public Works Loan Commissioners and successfully lobbied hard on his behalf. William was sworn in on 10 January 1855, initially with a salary of £1,200.

Leaving his boys at Barn Hey, William moved to London. He first stayed with his parents-in-law at 17 (now 1) Hyde Park Street. Their tenant next door was willing to move out and so William moved into 16 (now 3) as his father-in-law's tenant. Some time in early 1856, the boys moved down from Liverpool to join their father after a year of being apart.[40]

Early drawing by HGW

November 1855,
aged 4 years 4 months

No. 3 Hyde Park Street
Paddington

Sketch of Eton College by HGW

8 March 1907

Chapter 2

School and University Days

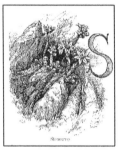

Stonecrop

oon after the boys' arrival in London from Liverpool, Willy had another change in his life: he was off to school in early April 1856. Unlike shy and delicate Henry, Willy was a daring and hardy boy, so perhaps he took all of it in his stride.

Back in the nursery in Hyde Park Street, Henry was not left to his own devices. His first governess arrived in June 1856, just before his fifth birthday. This was Miss Jane Treherne, a very kind and gentle lady, with whom Henry remained in touch until her death. Henry was also sent to French classes with a M. Roche, which he enjoyed thoroughly, and a dancing class, which he disliked very much! [41]

Then in January 1860, aged 8½, Henry followed Willy to boarding school, joining him at Callipers, in Chipperfield Common, near Watford:

The REV. C. A. JOHNS, B.A., F.L.S., late Master of Helston Grammar School, EDUCATES, for the Public Schools, &c., TWELVE BOYS under 14 years of age, who are treated in all respects as members of his own family. References of the highest order. Residence in a high and healthy part of Herts. Terms, 100 Guineas.
CALLIPERS HALL, RICKMANSWORTH [42]

Rev. Charles Alexander Johns was a well-known naturalist and a fellow of the Linnean Society. Henry remembered him as a "very good teacher generally" who had the "gift of inspiring all nature study with interest." [43]

Callipers Hall was a well-situated large Georgian house. A few years before, the Hall was described in an advertisement in the *Morning Post*:

> CALLIPERS HALL, situate in the parish of Watford, near Chipperfield-common, in the county of Herts, and within three miles of the railway station, consisting of a very comfortable residence, approached by a lodge entrance, in excellent repair, and containing every convenience for the occupation of a respectable family, with stabling and coach house, lawn, pleasure grounds, and kitchen garden... [44]

An old postcard from the period shows it to be three floors high, with four windows across the front on the first and second floor. Johns was something of a progressive thinker, shown by the installation of a gymnasium and baths at the school.[45]

Henry lived here with Rev. and Mrs. Johns, their daughter Ann, and up to fifteen other boys – no longer just the twelve boys as in the advertisement above; the school was growing. Arthur Evans, an exact contemporary (born two days before Henry), attended Callipers Hall while Henry was there. Evans went on to be one of the foremost archaeologists of the age, excavating the palace of Knossos on Crete. They parted ways when Evans went to Harrow, and Henry to Eton, but then went up to Oxford University at the same time in 1870, even attending the same College. In fact, Henry kept in contact with almost all his contemporaries at Callipers. In July 1914, for a fiftieth anniversary of their leaving the school, he brought together five of the six old boys who left at the same time as he did, Arthur Evans among them.[46]

In September 1862 Henry, aged 11, gained his first experience of staying abroad. By this time, Willy had left Callipers and had become a Naval Cadet, having moved to a "crammer's school" in Fareham to pass into the Navy. Willy, Henry and their father went to stay with the Nicholls grandparents, who were holidaying in Dover, and their father decided to take the boys over to Calais for a couple of nights.[47]

Soon after this, Willy was posted to HMS *Sutlej*, sailing on 11 December 1862 for the Pacific and, as it turned out, not returning home for five years. Henry wrote: "When Willy came home we were both so changed that we did not know each other."[48]

Henry's school continued to grow and when its roll was twenty-five boys the accommodation at Callipers Hall was no longer suitable. In September 1863 – for Henry's final year there – the school moved to Winton House on the edge of Winchester. The boys regretted the move, exchanging the open spaces of Chipperfield Common for a city.[49]

Having left Winton House in July 1864, Henry accompanied his father on a holiday to Cornwall, exploring Nicholls family roots. The holiday was extended into September when they were invited by the Tower family to stay with them in Tresco in the Scilly Isles.[50] Brownlow Tower was one of Henry's school friends at Callipers/ Winton House.

Soon after returning from this holiday, on Wednesday 21 September 1864, Henry arrived at Eton for his "first half." Henry was in Vidal's House, named after Rev. F. Vidal.[51] His Tutor there was William Johnson (later known as William Cory), at this time in his early 40s and who had been an assistant master at Eton for almost 20 years. Nicknamed "Tute" by his students, Johnson made a significant impact on the school. He was described as "the most brilliant Eton tutor of his day"[52] and "W. J. of all I have ever known was by heaven the most supremely gifted."[53]

Apart from being awarded the Prince Consort's French prize in November 1868,[54] Henry's successes at Eton were sporting rather than academic. After appearing first as cox in *Defiance*, one of the Lower Boats in 1867,[55] Henry was promoted to cox of the first Upper Boat, the *Monarch*, in June the following year.[56] That month he also coxed the College Eight and one of the Upper Fours boats.[57]

Henry achieved House Colours for football, but an accident in a football game in November 1868 put an end both to his football and ultimately to his serious rowing. It was then that he took up both "Eton fives" and fencing.[58] In the latter he became very accomplished as we shall see.

In summer 1869 Henry was aged 18 and about to start his final year at Eton. Despite his injury, he got into "the boats" as a rower, albeit in one of the Lower Boats – the *Defiance* again.[59] He completed his time at Eton by being head of his house, and reaching the "second division." [60]

At Eton, Henry developed his artistic abilities. He was taught by the gifted Sam Evans,[61] who had been Drawing Master at Eton since 1854. Trained in Paris and at the Royal Academy Schools, Evans had been elected as an Associate of the Royal Watercolour Society in 1859. He was an inspirational teacher who clearly found in Henry a ready response. The family remembered a comment made to the young Henry by Sam Evans about Henry's artistic talent: "Well, young man, your bread is buttered for life." [62]

Henry was awarded "First Drawing Prize" twice in his Eton career, the second time being in his final year.[63] We shall encounter Henry's art works throughout this book, including the capitals at the beginning of each chapter, taken from a book he illustrated.

Henry left Eton in the summer of 1870, and matriculated at Brasenose College, Oxford, on 9 June, to study Classics and History.[64] While at Oxford, Henry became a proficient fencer. In 1872, he won the University Foils competition, "displaying great quickness and agility." [65] Henry kept up his interest in fencing, winning an even bigger competition in 1886 and later illustrating a book on fencing.

It is at this point that we must consider Henry's favourite sport and leisure activity, mountaineering. Although there had been many throughout medieval history and beyond who had ascended mountains for more than simply getting from A to B, the popular sport of mountaineering had really only begun around 1850, with the famous Alpine Club being formed in 1857.

From 6 to 29 August 1866 Henry (aged 15) accompanied his father on what was for Henry his first trip to the Alps. They journeyed from Martigny in Switzerland to Chamonix in France, ascending Brévent, then across the Col de la Seigne into Italy, arriving at Courmayeur, then finally over the Théodule Pass to Zermatt, Switzerland. Then they travelled back to Boulogne via Zurich, Strasbourg and Paris. [66] Henry formed the habit of keeping an illustrated journal of his trips which became the basis of much of his later drawing and his lectures on Alpine Mountaineering.

Their next summer holiday began with a visit to seek out family in the Netherlands. They stayed with William's first cousin Daniel Willink van Collen at "Gunterstein," a remarkable moated castle in Breukelen (that is now open to the public). The family could live in such magnificence because Daniel had married an heiress, Johanna van Collen, in 1844, adding her family name to his. Johanna had died in 1853, leaving Daniel and 2 sons and 3 daughters, all around Henry's age. The youngest daughter, Albertine, later married Louis Quarles van Ufford, whom we shall meet again further on in Henry's story.

Leaving Gunterstein, they made their way across the Netherlands to Willink Hof, near Winterswyk not far from the German border, a 16th century house, now a farmhouse, which

Gunterstein

HGW's drawing
dated 17 April 1887

was the earliest known location associated with the Willink family. They met there an old farmer and his wife, whose maiden name had indeed been Willink.

Willy accompanied his father and brother, having returned just a month previously from his five-year absence on the *Sutlej*. Perhaps because he had been so long from home, Willy was not a happy traveller. Henry described his brother as:

> a young man of twenty, with no particular hobby and no knowledge of local or general history, or manners and customs of continental life. He cared little for reading and picture galleries and architecture and scenery, and did not sketch. He preferred theatres and cafés, and music under the trees, and bright young companions of both sexes, and so on.[67]

The three Willinks then crossed Germany to Kiel and on to Copenhagen, then Christiana (now known as Oslo) and finally Stockholm. Henry liked the Scandinavian scenery and returned to the region several times throughout his life.

You had to be a patient and unhurried traveller in those days. Starting back, they caught a train from Stockholm to Malmo, which had a journey time of 34 hours; it is now accomplished in about 4½!

Soon after their return to London, Willy was posted as sub-lieutenant on HMS *Pallas*, on which he had just one Mediterranean voyage. In 1869, he transferred to HMS *Eclipse*, bound for Bermuda, and various Canadian and American ports. This proved to be an unhappy time, with Willy seeming to get into trouble with the Captain frequently.[68]

In 1868, Henry and his father were again in the Alps. This was a longer stay than in 1866, totalling twenty-nine nights abroad. Henry detailed the itinerary:

> Brussels, Bonn, up the Rhine to Frankfurt, Heidelberg, Basle, Glarus (near to which place we had a narrow escape from death,

our *einspanner* horse having shied badly, and only just failed to tip us over the unguarded edge of a precipice), Elm, via the Martins-Loch, Flims, Ilanz (in the Romansch country), Andermatt (by the Furka), Rhone Glacier, Rosenlaui, Grindelwald, Lauterbrunnen (where we met the John Orreds), Mürren (Schilthorn), Interlaken, Berne, Neuchâtel, Dijon, Fontainebleau (where we saw the Prince Imperial, hunting in the forest), and, finally, Paris.[69]

Making use of the legend of dragons living in the Alps, Henry later drew the Grindelwald glacier as a *Wilderwurm* – see opposite. Henry particularly loved this area of the Bernese Oberland, with the Wetterhorn mountain, looming over the village of Grindelwald, being his especial favourite.

Henry's diary gives a good description of his father's mode of dress while on the mountains: "a black frock coat and white top hat with a green veil, and on serious occasions a rope, in case of need, was added and wound around his waist." [70]

John Orred, mentioned above in Henry's itinerary, had married Henry's father's sister, Catharina Mary Willink, in 1843. Catharina died in 1858, aged 40, leaving her husband with eight children. John married again in 1862, to Frances Hilton. John had the distinction sometime later to be presented with a certificate by the Guides of the Bureau of Chamonix stating that he was the fattest traveller they had ever taken up Mont Blanc! The family lived at Ashwicke Hall, Marshfield, north of Bath. Henry liked to visit his cousins there, and made many sketches of the house and area.

Henry and his father returned to Switzerland the following year, 1869, with their longest tour, starting with London to Berne by boat and train. Then, mostly on foot from Kandersteg and the Gemmi Pass to Leukerbad, Visp and Viesch, and so to the Eggishorn. Bad weather delayed their trek, but they eventually made it to Saas. From there they took the Monte Moro Pass and so passed into Italy and on to Macugnaga in Piedmont.

Wilderwurm Gletscher.

HGW's illustration of the
Grindelwald Glacier,
personified as a dragon, or *Wilderwurm*.

HGW's illustration "On the Messer Grat"
- showing the clothes generally
worn by Victorian Mountaineers

They continued over the Barranva Pass ("five hours to the top, three hours down") to Fobello. They then drove to Varallo and via the Colma Pass to Lake Orta. They spent some days as ordinary tourists around Como and Milan. Unfortunately, Henry was incapacitated for two days due to a surfeit of grapes!

They continued their journey by carriage and steamer then carriage again: Morbegno, Sondrio, Pirno, Le Prese, Bernina Pass, Pontresina, Samaden, Tarasp, Martinsbruck and Finstermünz, just into Austria. Through much of this journey, Henry's father William was not well.

They stopped "three nights at Munich, followed by one each at Nuremberg, Bamberg, Frankfurt (two) and Wiesbaden and Cologne, [which] brought us to Holland again." [71]

They spent time with family in the Netherlands, but William was keen to get home as he felt so unwell, so they proceeded to Rotterdam. Henry later wrote:

> On reaching Rotterdam we found, to our horror, that we should have to go on by steamer via Dordrecht and Möerdyke, where there was not then (nor for some years afterwards) any bridge. The small river steamer lay a hundred yards from the railway station; the wind and rain were positively awful; and we were a soaking wet crowd that scrambled on board at Rotterdam and proceeded to get food. We passed Dordrecht all right, and along the little Spey, from the mouth of which we could see the train by which we were to proceed, waiting for us on the opposite shore. And the hurricane was still alarming, blowing up stream, against ebb-tide. Pilot went up-stream a little, to allow for tide, and in order to enter the little harbour: but it carried us past the entrance into shallow water, the boat refusing to answer the helm, and we ran aground. Rather a heavy sea, but after some bumping we got off and tried again, similar result except that we were rather further off. The vessel heeled over and began to bump more than ever. The windows of the saloon crashed and the sea began to pour in. Ladies rushed on deck and there was great confusion... We really thought it was all up. But somehow,

we did get off, with more bumps, into deep water, though the stream and the wind were so strong that we could not steer. And eventually the skipper concluded to give up and took us back to the Spey, where we made fast ignominiously to a tree! There we spent a wretched night, as the cabin was all drenched. The next morning the weather had abated, and we cast off about 5.30 and crossed safely to Möerdyke, where we waited for an hour for a train, and eventually proceeded by Rosendaal and Antwerp to Brussels…" [72]

By this time, William was feverish and very ill indeed. They travelled by land on to Calais and took ship to Dover. On reaching home, William was unable to stir from bed for many days. He never went abroad again.[73]

The summer holiday in the following year was therefore in Britain – at Fodderty Lodge, Dingwall, in Scotland. Henry, his father, his Aunt Georgiana and two cousins – Mary and Harriet ("Harry") Ouvry – formed the party. Henry had been given a new gun by his father, and so especially enjoyed the shooting parties.[74]

Soon after their return south, Henry's brother Willy unexpectedly left the navy and arrived home. He had been unhappy with his position on HMS *Eclipse* under a captain with whom he could not get on. Willy's future was uncertain for a while.[75]

Henry continued to explore Great Britain, with a visit to Snowdonia in 1871 and his first visit to the Lake District in 1872. The latter was undertaken shortly after a long Austrian walking tour with two undergraduate friends, from Linz on the Danube to Villach. He arrived back home on 30 July, and was in Windermere with Willy on 5 August.[76]

In an article called "Lakeland Memories," written 55 years later, Henry wrote of this trip:

Our first peak was Gummer's How! Knapsacks on backs we straggled carelessly for ten or eleven delightful days about

Lakeland. We looked for the darkest shadings in the Ordnance map, and just went for those parts, very casual, very unintelligent, and not very daring, but finding our own way regardless of paths, and eschewing roads as much as possible. Of course we bagged the highest tops, High Street, Helvellyn, Skiddaw, Scawfell (sic) Pike, Langdale Pikes, etc. I remember walking right round Wastwater, by myself, one afternoon, my brother's feet being sore – we were always getting sore feet, but I had brought a seasoned pair of feet from abroad. I found the screes discomfortable. We had lots of "bad" weather, cloudy and very wet...

We did not like Wastwater (Huntsman's Inn) much; for they did not dry our clothes and never called us in the morning; so we could not get off till 7-15! Incredible as in these days it may seem, we used to aim at being called at 5-30. And we lived plain, even if we did not think high. Our daily bill used to average about 10/- each, *tout compris*, beer and all.[77]

In 1873, before settling down to his chosen career, Henry had a busy year in the mountains, with visits to the Cuillin Hills on Skye, the Pyrenees and the Swiss Alps (twice!). The list was rounded off with another visit to the Lake District.[78]

Henry completed his Oxford degree, graduating as B.A. in the Third Class in Modern History. This became, in due course, an M.A. in 1877.[79]

In 1873, Henry swapped the spires of Oxford for the Courts of Lincoln's Inn in central London and the study of Law.

Henry's sketch of his brother Willy

On Cader Idris, 1 May 1878

Chapter 3

Life in London

Alpenrose

arely does family life stand still. During Henry's school and University days, his four grandparents had all died. [80]

The 1861 census showed the Willink family and the Nicholls family living next door to each other – the former at 16 Hyde Park Street, Paddington, and the latter at number 17.[81]

By 1871, with the deaths of both Sir George and Harriet, there was no longer a Nicholls household. The Willink family's house, renumbered by this date to 3 Hyde Park Street, was now owned by Georgiana Nicholls, Henry's unmarried aunt. Aunt Georgie, as she was known, joined the Willink household at number 3 with William becoming joint occupier and tenant.[82]

Henry had of course not known a mother's love. His "Grandmamma Willink" had lovingly cared for him until he was aged 5, but she had been left behind in Liverpool and had now died. Perhaps, to some extent, his Aunt Georgie took a sort of mother's role for him now that he was a young man. He described Aunt Georgie in his father's biography:

> She was a woman of strong character, a staunch friend with a warm heart, and a marked sense of duty. She ran the household with care and economy, perhaps rather on the "sparing side," for

she hated waste and irregularity. She was fond of society and of reading, especially history and biography. She enjoyed easy travelling until late in life, and had the kind habit of taking one or other of her nieces or other young girl friends to Switzerland with her for a month in the summer, making neat little sketches wherever she went. She and I were very fond of each other, and could agree to disagree without the least friction upon many subjects.[83]

Henry had enrolled at Lincoln's Inn on 9 November 1872 while still at Oxford.[84] Compulsory bar exams had recently been instituted, although the current Lincoln's Inn website states that the exams could be passed "by anyone with a modicum of application with a few weeks' study"! [85]

As well as following the course of study to become a barrister, it is likely that it was around this time that Henry enrolled and studied at the Slade School of Art. Established in 1871 with Sir Edward Poynton as the first Slade Professor, the school became quickly known for its standard of fine art teaching and its enrolment of women on the same terms as men. Kate Greenaway, the children's book author, was a student there at much the same time. According to his daughter's memoir of her father, Henry was later elected as a member of the Royal Watercolour Society.[86] However, the Society have been unable to substantiate the claim.

In 1875 Henry joined the Inns of Court Volunteers, that is the 23rd Middlesex (Inns of Court) Rifle Volunteer Corps. This Corps was sometimes known as "the Devil's Own," an appellation given by George III in 1803 when told that it was composed entirely of lawyers! Henry remained part of this volunteer corps until 1893, and over those 18 years moved through the ranks from Private to Captain.[87]

The examinations for the Bar, whether easy or difficult, took place on the last two days of December 1876 and the first four days of the new year. At this sitting, 87 "gentlemen" entered for English Law, Henry being among the 49 who passed.[88] He was then formally called to the Bar at Lincoln's Inn on 26 January 1877.[89] He practised at the Chancery Bar until 1884.[90]

During his short legal career, he also tried his hand at journalism. From 1880 to 1882 he contributed to the *Weekly Reporter*, moving on to the *Law Times* for whom he reported on chancery cases from 1882 to at least 1885. He also produced drawings for *Punch* magazine on a regular basis from about 1875.[91]

Henry considered 1875 to be his first year of serious mountaineering. In company with his brother Willy and his cousin Harry Latham, he ascended the Wetterhorn (3,692 m) and Titlis (3,283 m) mountains in Switzerland. In subsequent years, he climbed the Matterhorn (4,478 m), Breithorn (4,164 m), Galenstock (3,586 m), Oberalpstock (3,328 m) and the Mönch (4,107 m). He and his companions had a narrow escape from an avalanche on an expedition to conquer the Finsteraahorn (4,274 m), the highest mountain in the Bernese Alps.[92]

Catharine, Henry's daughter, later wrote of him:

> Willink's mountaineering interests did not lie so much with the big peaks, though he was undoubtedly a good rock-climber with a good eye for a route and with good hands and feet, as is shown by his account of certain unaccompanied climbs up the Pillar Rock and Tryfaen. His love of mountains was more of an exploratory kind, and making passes from valley to valley attracted him more than big mountain expeditions. Nothing gave him more pleasure at any time than to have an excuse to pore over a map, and his diaries show that he rarely stopped for more than two days in the same place. Hill country anywhere always attracted him, and besides the Alps he visited the Pyrenees and made a journey across Sweden and Norway in days when travelling was much more difficult than it is at present. The Lakes and North Wales he loved and knew intimately at all seasons and in all weathers.[93]

"No. 1: Hallo – here's a bo…"

"No. 2: …g !!"

Sketches by HGW

Pillar Rock: The Great Chimney
by HGW.
Dated 16 August 1877

In August 1877 Henry was back in the Lake District. This time he was in the company of his brother Willy, his cousin Edmund (known as Eddy) Wingfield, and friend (later brother-in-law) Gerard Clark. Pillar Rock (892 m) was the most interesting climb, and Henry produced a drawing of it, a version of which he later included in his *Lakeland Memories* article – see opposite.[94] It looks in the illustration as if the upper climber is making notes, or more probably sketching. Maybe it is a self-portrait. If so, perhaps Henry should have shown the "sizable brick-shaped stone" that he accidentally set loose and that narrowly missed his cousin Eddy's head below!

The small notebook that the upper climber is holding is a good illustration of the type of sketch book that Henry habitually carried. At 7" by 4" by ¾" thick (approximately 18cm by 10cm by 2cm), a sketch book could fit into a pocket, and Henry made sure he never went anywhere without one.

Henry's brother, Willy, had been without a career following his departure from the navy in 1870. His father decided that Willy, like Henry, should become a lawyer. After much work with several coaches, Willy was successful and was called to the Bar, at the Inner Temple, just five months after his brother in June 1877.[95] Henry wrote later that he believed that, despite being set up in chambers, Willy never actually received any case to work on.[96]

Henry and Willy toured Sweden, Norway and Russia, setting out on 12 July 1878 and not returning until 15 September. Henry filled a sketchbook with over 30 drawings from this visit. Their itinerary included Oslo, Stockholm, St. Petersburg, Trondheim, Lapland, Bergen and Stavanger. Henry's drawings were not just of mountains, but of people, animals, houses, and boats.

Millwall Docks
12 July 1878

Stockholm, Sweden
19 July 1878

Lapp Hut near Skalstugan, Sweden
2 August 1878

Head of Nordfjord, Norway
21 August 1878

In London, there were many visits to 3 Hyde Park Street by first cousins. The Ouvry sisters (Mary and Harry) were the most frequent, and Henry was close to both sisters. The Wingfields were next – Sophie, Eddy, Cecilia (known as Lily) and Gertrude. Then there were the Orreds (Annie, Edith, Katie, Woodville, Randal and Sophia); the Willinks (Arthur and Willy); and the Nicholls (Agnes, Emily, Harriet, Lina, George and Henry).

The Wingfields were the children of the Rev. William Wingfield and Charlotte (sister of Henry's mother). Six months after their marriage, William Wingfield left the Church of England and became Roman Catholic. This had upset Charlotte's parents, George and Harriet Nicholls, who felt that consent had been given to the marriage with no indication of change of religion in the offing.[97]

However, time often heals rifts. In this case, with the deaths of Sir George Nicholls in 1865, his wife Harriet in 1869 and then William Wingfield in 1874, the families were back on visiting terms. Then the ties became even closer, as in November 1878 first cousins William Nicholls Willink and Cecilia Jane Frances de Chantal Wingfield married – or, as the families would have said, Willy married Lily.[98]

Henry had stepped into a family tradition in 1876 by joining the committee of Birmingham Canal Navigations. The first family connection with this company had been through Henry's grandfather Nicholls.

George Nicholls had been involved in the development of canals since the 1820s. As previously mentioned, he had been the superintendent of the Gloucester and Berkeley Canal. He became a shareholder in the Birmingham Canal Navigations company initially in order to promote canal connections between Birmingham and Gloucester.

George briefly joined the committee of Birmingham Canal Navigations in 1834, before other responsibilities took him away to London. He then rejoined the committee in 1844, continuing thereafter for 20 years and becoming its chairman from 1853.

In 1864, George (by now Sir George) retired from the chairmanship and was succeeded in that position by his son-in-law, William Williamson Willink, although Sir George continued to attend meetings until his death just a year later.[99]

Henry's father had become a member of the committee around 1852, not long after becoming a widower. By 1876, having been chairman for 12 years, he resigned from the committee due to failing health. At the meeting in Daimler House, Paradise Street, Birmingham, when his resignation from the Board was announced, Henry was elected to the committee in his place.[100] This began Henry's association with the Company which was to last over 60 years.[101]

Birmingham Canal Navigations was incorporated in 1768 and, while not the only canal operator in the Birmingham area, it was the most important. At the time that Henry joined the committee, it was an improving company with its annual turnover being £231,935 4s 4d, a 12% increase from the year before. The company owned and managed about 160 miles of canal in the Birmingham area; about 100 miles of this network is still in use and in the company's hands. Henry travelled regularly to Birmingham for the monthly meetings. In 1906 Henry became Vice Chairman of the company,[102] and often found himself chairing meetings. Under his chairmanship, meetings were not exactly prolonged. For example:

> A one-minute meeting took place in Birmingham today. This was the time it took the proprietors of the Birmingham Canal Navigations to transact their business at the annual meeting today.
>
> They started as "Big Brum" commenced to chime the hour, and concluded just after the last note of twelve died away. The "hustle" took place at the offices in Daimler House. Mr. Henry George Willink presided.

39

> The report and accounts for the past year were presented and approved. It was decided that a dividend at the rate of £2 for each sum of £100 consolidated stock for the half-year ended 3 December, subject to the deduction of income tax, should be paid to the proprietors on 15 March next.
>
> The following gentlemen were elected members of the committee for the ensuing year: Messrs. Henry Valentine Bache de Sagte, Owen F. Grazebrook, Alfred Charles Lyon, George Robert Jebb, and Henry George Willink. Messrs. Howard Smith, Slocombe, and Co. were re-elected auditors.[103]

It is hard to believe that all this business could be achieved within the time it took the city's clock to chime twelve times. However, the next half yearly meeting – also chaired by Henry – was similarly reported to have lasted less than a minute, so Henry must have made it his aim to accomplish the work in this way! [104]

Henry's association with Birmingham Canal Navigations, as has been said, stretched to over 60 years. He was presented with an address on parchment in 1935 (when he was aged 84) on his completion of 60 years' service – a remarkable achievement.[105] Henry was still Vice Chairman of the company at the time of his death in 1938, having held that post therefore for 32 years of his 62 – almost 63 – years of service on the committee.

The association between the Willink family and Birmingham Canal Navigations continued to a fourth generation with Henry's son Francis. Francis joined his father on the committee in the late 1930s and continued as a member until 1949.

*****

The top of the Matterhorn

HGW's watercolour, dated 30 August 1879

With Willy married, 3 Hyde Park Street became again home to just the three – William, Aunt Georgie, and Henry. About the time of Willy's marriage, Henry began to have such thoughts too. In 1936, Henry wrote:

> It was no sudden affection that brought Mary and me together. Nor at first was it a case of love on both sides, for although we had known each other from childhood the idea of marriage came later, and when she realized the change in me this occasioned none in her. Indeed, I had for three or four years been longing that she would change her mind, and give my father a second daughter-in-law. For a long time, however, she allowed me no hope. Eventually, at the end of October, 1879, she yielded so far as to say that she would give me a final answer in six months if I still wished it.
>
> They were very long months, but the 1st May, 1880, came at last – and I had *not* changed *my* mind. My father, who loved both her and her sister "Harry" dearly, gave his consent and so did their father… Words cannot tell what our union has meant to me and our children during the thirty-eight years (1880 to 1918) of our happy married life. Her influence has helped and inspired me from first to last.[106]

On Thursday 9 September 1880, Henry married Mary Grace Ouvry at Wing Church, Buckinghamshire, where Mary's father, Rev. Peter T. Ouvry, was incumbent.[107] *The Bucks Herald* reported:

> Thursday was ushered in by merry peals from the church bells, which were continued at intervals during the day, and at the hour appointed for the ceremony (half-past eleven) the approaches to the church and the building itself were thronged with interested spectators. The interior was tastefully decorated for the occasion with flowers, ferns, moss, etc., some choice plants being kindly lent for the purpose by Mr. Leopold de Rothschild. The bride, who was led into church and given away by Colonel Ouvry C.B., her uncle, wore an ivory satin dress, trimmed with lace, a real

orange-blossom and myrtle wreath, and tulle veil, and carried a splendid bouquet. She was attended by five bridesmaids, Misses Harriet, Constance, Francisca, Aimee, and Ethel Ouvry, who were attired in dresses of cream coloured Indian muslin, trimmed with lace; straw hats, trimmed with lace and red roses, and each of whom carried a handsome bouquet of red roses… Mr. Charles Phillips was best man…

The marriage ceremony was performed by the bride's father, the Rev. P. T. Ouvry, appropriate hymns and chants being sung by the choir, Mr. H. Caves presiding at the organ, and playing the Wedding March as the bride and bridegroom left the church after the close of the service. Flowers were strewn on their path by members of the congregation.

Breakfast was served in a tent on the vicarage lawn by Mr. J. J. Woods of Leighton Buzzard… The bride and bridegroom left early in the afternoon for London en route to Switzerland and Italy to spend their honeymoon.[108]

The Luton Times and Advertiser added that, as the couple left "for the honeymoon, and, as they drove in an open carriage along the street leading to Leighton, flowers and rice were completely showered upon them from the doors and windows of the houses on either side."[109]

With Henry being recently elected to the Alpine Club,[110] perhaps it was not too surprising to find the happy couple honeymooning in the Swiss and Italian Alps. I wonder how much mountaineering Mary did. An article in the *Alpine Journal* in 1983 describes a gift by D. T. Pilkington to the Alpine Club of what they call a characteristic work by H. G. Willink: "a real treasure in the form of a sketch book recording an alpine and Italian tour in 1880. It contains about 50 delightful watercolour sketches."[111] This is most likely to have been Henry's sketch book from their honeymoon.

Like Willy and Lily, Henry and Mary were first cousins. Their mothers were three daughters of George and Harriet Nicholls: Charlotte, Jane and Catharine. Charlotte, who had married William Wingfield, was the mother of Lily (Cecilia).

Jane, who had married the Rev. P. T. Ouvry, was the mother of Mary. Catharine, who had married William Williamson Willink, was the mother of Willy and Henry.[112]

HGW's watercolour of
Mary Grace Ouvry playing the organ
in Wing Church, Buckinghamshire

Dated 22 April 1876

Back in London, Henry continued with his career as a barrister-at-law with offices at 8, New Court, Lincoln's Inn,[113] and with his involvement in the Inns of Court Rifle Volunteers. In 1881 Henry became a Lieutenant, and it was while he held this rank that he won the officers' fencing competition at the Royal Military Tournament. The first Tournament was held at the Agricultural Hall, Islington, London, in June 1880, being "a Military Tournament and Assault-at-Arms" with 53 separate Competitions.[114] It was in the seventh annual Tournament that Henry was successful:

> In fencing, there was a keen struggle for supremacy between regulars and auxiliaries. Two accomplished and graceful swordsmen of the Coldstream Guards held their own well until nearly to the finish; but first Captain Codrington and the Lieut. G. R. Smith were vanquished by the less finished but more agile attacks of Lieutenant H. G. Willink, who finally bore off the Champions Prize and gained glory for himself and the "Devil's Own" volunteers.[115]

Henry kept up his fencing for many years. In an article in the *Alpine Journal* in 1943, Geoffrey Winthrop Young looked back to the previous century and wrote of Henry and his great friend Clinton Dent: "He and Willink were fine fencers, among their many talents, and when I was introducing fencing into Eton at the end of the century, I used to get them down for exhibition bouts."[116]

Henry applied his artistic talents as well as his fencing abilities for the Inns of Court Rifle Volunteers as "for many years he drew the amusing and original designs for the programme for the Annual Assault-at-Arms."[117] In a similar way, he designed the menus for many Alpine Club dinners.[118] Henry was also beginning to make his name as an illustrator. As well as producing illustrations for the *Alpine Journal* (frequently from 1886) and *Punch*, he had a drawing printed in the June edition of Cassell's *The Magazine of Arts* – a specially commissioned illustration for "The Two Painters," a poem by Austin Dobson. [119]

Henry and Mary had barely settled into their new home, 29 Albion Street (which was very close to 3 Hyde Park Street) when, on 11 January 1881, Henry's father had a stroke. This paralysed him so that was unable to move from his bed and severely affected his mental capacity. He did gradually recover some mental faculties, but was never the man he had been. [120]

Henry, Mary and Aunt Georgie shared the responsibilities for his care, together with a nurse. In the 1881 census, Henry and Mary are recorded as visitors at 3 Hyde Park Street, Paddington, showing that despite living so close they spent the night there too when needed. [121]

Shortly before noon on 11 December 1883 William Williamson Willink died at 3 Hyde Park Street, aged 75. He was buried four days later at St. Michael's Church, Huyton, Liverpool, where his wife had been buried 32 years earlier. [122] Henry wrote:

> I saw his coffin laid beside hers and the tiny one which contained the remains of my poor little sister, Harriet, whom I never saw, and whose death had meant so much to them. The sight of the three coffins lying there together, at last, brought strangely home to me the fact that my mother and my sister had really and truly existed. [123]

In January, the will was proved:

> The will (dated November 23, 1878) with codicil (dated July 21, 1879), of Mr. William Williamson Willink, late of No. 3 Hyde Park-street, who died on December 11 last, has been proved by Henry George Willink (son) and Miss Georgiana Elizabeth Nicholls (sister-in-law), the executors, the value of the personal estate amounting to above £147,000. The testator leaves £100 Consols to the official trustees of charitable funds, in trust for

the poor of the parishes of Huyton and Roby, near Liverpool, and legacies of £1,000 each to his brothers and sisters-in-law or their families. Besides other legacies to servants and to others (including one to his cousin Jan Abraham Willink) he further bequeaths to Miss G. E. Nicholls [Aunt Georgie], for her life, his household furniture, plate and effects, and £10,000 Birmingham Canal Stock. The residue of his personal property he leaves to his two sons, William Nicholls Willink and Henry George Willink.[124]

With his share of his father's estate, Henry was now very comfortably off.

On 9 July 1884, the day before Henry's 33rd birthday, Henry and Mary began their family life with the birth of a son: John Ouvry Willink.[125] The following year, John contracted meningitis, and ten days later – on 13 June 1885 – he died, aged 11 months.

Baby John was buried at St. Mary's, Acton, four days later, following a funeral taken by Mary's father, the Rev. P. T. Ouvry.[126] Henry and Mary's daughter Catharine wrote, following her father's death in 1938, that this bereavement remained so acute that the parents could hardly speak of it.[127]

A week after John died, Henry's sister-in-law, Lily, gave birth to her and Willy's first (and in the event, only) child – Thomas Wingfield Willink.[128]

Henry and Mary decided soon after John's death to move house from 29 Albion Street. Their choice was 1 Hyde Park Street, where Henry's grandparents had lived (then called No. 17) and next door to the house where Henry grew up, still occupied by Aunt Georgie.

At 1 Hyde Park Street, on 15 October 1885, Mary gave birth to their second child: Catharine Dorothy Willink, known in the family as Katie. Catharine was baptised by her grandfather, Rev. P. T. Ouvry, at St. John's Church, Paddington, just a short walk up Hyde Park Street, on 25 November 1885.[129]

HGW's quick sketch of his baby son,
John Ouvry Willink

Sketch dated 20 July 1884

In early 1886 Henry wrote an illustrated article for
Longman's Magazine entitled "Map-flapping," describing a
method for transmitting details of a sketch or photograph
using Morse code.[130] This was a method developed by Henry
and another Lieutenant in the Inns of Court Volunteers (14th
Middlesex), Alexander Glen.

Glen read a paper entitled "The Transmission of Drawings
by Signal" to a meeting of the Royal United Service
Institution on 22 January 1886. Glen said that:

The object of the system … was that one person who had the
means of communicating with another by telegraph, heliograph,
lamp, flag, or other mode of signalling, might enable the

recipient of the signals to make a fac-simile (sic) of any drawing which might be in the hands of the sender...

The drawing was divided by actual or imaginary lines into columns of a certain breadth, and into rows of the same breadth at right angles to the columns.

Thus, a co-ordinate grid system was set up and a code used with groups of letters to indicate features placed on the map. The code included methods to designate buildings and other features. Glen continued:

A straight line joining two points was denoted by joining in one group the two pairs of letters which denoted these points. A line passing through a series of points was denoted by a series of groups which denoted those points... A curved line was denoted by indicating as many points on it as the degree of accuracy might demand.[131]

Glen and Henry had carried out various trials of the system, which had met with considerable success. On 18 April 1885, they had succeeded in transmitting by flag across Wimbledon Common the plan of the battle of Hasheen that had taken place three weeks earlier. The claim was that this method could be accomplished in a "comparatively short space of time". However, it does not seem to have become a commonly used method, and so perhaps it was rather more time-consuming than they had hoped.

All this practice of his signalling skills meant that Henry was certainly well prepared for his Army Signalling exam. It was reported that:

Several Volunteer officers have just passed an examination in Army signalling, which has been held at Wellington Barracks. Most of them came out of the ordeal in an exceedingly creditable manner, Lieutenant Willink, of the "Inns of Court," gaining 98 per cent of the highest number of points.[132]

Lieutenant Willink was also a member of the Home District Tactical and War Game Society. In November 1886, Henry took a leading role in one of these games:

> The first War Game of the Season of the Home District Tactical and War Game Society was played last evening at the Westminster Town Hall, in the presence of Colonel Julian H. Hall, Colonel G. H. Moncrieff, Colonel Sterling, and a large number of officers of the Regular and Auxiliary Forces. The players for "Red" were – Colonel Clark, 1st V. B. Royal Fusiliers, and Lieutenant Willink, 14th Middlesex (Inns of Court) R. V.; and for "Blue" – Major Ridge and Colonel Spiers, 20th Middlesex (Artists) R. V. Colonel Lonsdale Hale, late R. E., was chief umpire, and the assistant umpires were – For "Red" Lieut. Colonel Farrell, 3d V. B. West Kent Regiment; and for "Blue," Captain Canning, Queen's Westminster R. V. The game was watched with much interest by the officers who were privileged to witness it. [133]

At the beginning of February 1888, Henry and Mary's second son, George Ouvry William Willink, was born. Like his sister, he was baptised by his grandfather, the Rev. P. T. Ouvry, at St. John's Church, Paddington. [134] That summer – from July to October – the family rented Wray Cottage beside Windermere. Henry wrote: "a golden time we had. Not only on the hills with relations and friends and alone, but sketching and boating, on lake and shore." [135]

His sketching was fast becoming of considerable note. An article on Mountaineering in *The Graphic* in 1889 contained 17 of Henry's sketches. The article stated:

> In spite of all the popularisation of the sport, people seem ignorant of what men really do when they go a-climbing. Mr. Willink's sketches are unexaggerated representations of some of the ordinary and some of the extraordinary incidents in such excursions… One sketch depicts an adventure which actually occurred on the Gabelhorn, near Zermatt, where three out of the

party of four, having been suddenly precipitated down the side of an *arête* by the breaking of a snow cornice, were held up by the rear guide (Ulrich Almer), and saved…

Our engravings of Mr. Willink's sketches are from photographs published by Messrs. William M. Spooner and Co., 379, Strand.[136]

Henry's sister-in-law, Lily, wife of Willy, died aged 33 after a few weeks' illness in March 1889. Several peals of muffled changes were rung in the Cradley parish church in token of respect, and the local newspaper wrote that "her welcome footsteps will be much missed at the door of the poor inhabitants around her part of the parish especially, where her kind disposition was constantly providing for their wants." [137] She left behind her husband and a son aged 3, Thomas Wingfield Willink. Tragically, William Nicholls Willink did not survive his wife long: he died aged 43 just two years later.[138]

In November 1889, the latest addition to the "All-England Series" sporting books was published by George Bell & Sons, on Fencing, written by H. A. Colmore Dunn and with illustrations by H. G. Willink I.C.S.A. (The initials after Henry's name stood for Inns of Court School of Arms.) [139]

Henry's 17 illustrations include types of equipment, grips and stances, followed by a series of diagrams showing attack and defensive moves. Below are a few examples from the book:

"Position of hand on foil (supination)"　　　　"Hand in pronation"

"On guard"   "Lunge"

"Parry of quarte"

"Riposte from parry of quarte"

Illustrations by HGW

Henry, who had been promoted from Lieutenant to Captain of the 14th Middlesex (Inns of Court) as of 1 January 1890,[140] and author H. A. Colmore Dunn were fellow members of the Inns of Court Rifle Volunteers. Soon after their collaboration on the book on Fencing, they were demonstrating their skills in fencing against each other in the sixth annual assault-of-arms of the Corps, which took place on 29 March 1890. The report of the event singled them out:

> In swordsmanship, England is still behindhand, compared with Continental countries; not that our best amateurs are not good, but – as in the case of the British Infantry, though with less reason – there are very few of them. Here again, the Inns of Court are fortunate, as the judicious spectator of Mr. WILLINK'S and Mr. DUNN'S fencing might easily have seen.
> Mr. DUNN is one of the very few Englishmen who have both studied the small-sword according to the exactness of the French school, and given their countrymen the benefit of their knowledge in a form easily understood by English readers.

Mr. WILLINK, as if to defy outrageously the warning of the old-fashioned lawyers against all exercise which is "violent or laborious," is not only a swordsman, but a mountaineer who is also an artist. His Alpine sketches combine fidelity with humour, and those who go to the Inns of Court Assault of Arms have a special reward in a programme adorned with some quaint device from his hand. This year a spirited portrait of the regimental fencing instructor appeared in the centre of a kind of bouquet of foils, masks and gloves.[141]

A few weeks before the fencing display above, Henry gave the first of many lectures on Alpine Climbing. The *Leighton Buzzard Observer and Linslade Gazette* carried the following advertisement:

LEIGHTON INSTITUTE.
THE NEXT LECTURE
will be given in the Assembly Room,
On Thursday, February 13th, 1890,
BY
H. G. WILLINK, ESQ.
Subject:
"ALPINE CLIMBING"
Illustrated with the Lantern.
The Chair will be taken at Eight O'clock p.m.,
by JOHN TINDALL, ESQ.
Admission- Members, Free;
Non-Members, First Seats 1s; Second Seats 6d.[142]

In the week following the lecture, this review appeared in the same newspaper:

On Thursday evening in last week, in connection with the Leighton Institute, H. G. Willink, Esq., delivered a most interesting lecture, on "Alpine Climbing," in the Assembly Room, to a large and appreciative audience.

John Tindall, Esq., presided, and introduced the lecturer as a personal friend, who was connected with the district of Leighton Buzzard by family ties, a member of the committee of the Alpine Club, and an accomplished observer, draughtsman, and mountaineer.

The lecture was illustrated with a series of beautiful views, from perfect photographs, reproduced on a screen by means of a powerful limelight lantern, manipulated by the master hand of Robt. Tindall, Esq.

Mr. Willink, remarking that comparatively few English people had seen a real mountain, no grander examples of which could be seen than among the Swiss Alps, proceeded to throw upon the screen a map of the mountainous district of Switzerland, showing the chief ranges, the direction of the valleys, the course of the chief rivers, and the district of eternal snow, together with splendid views of Mont Blanc...

He explained the formation of the moraines, or ridges of rocks, at the sides and centres of glaciers, and showed a marvellous picture of a glacier table or slab of rock balanced upon a pillar of ice...

Proceeding to the question of climbing, the lecturer commented on the outfit of the party – warm clothing, thick nailed-boots, ice-axe, rope, and blue spectacles... He then showed them the interior of a sleeping hut, with its rough accommodation and utensils, which were supposed to be left all clean and tidy for the next party; and passed to a beautiful drawing of his own, showing the start by lantern-light in the early dawn. Slide after slide succeeded, with admirably-drawn figures of the climbers, now consulting the compass, now cutting steps with the ice-axe, now creeping round places all but inaccessible; again descending with swift glissade, either erect or sitting, or using the rope for mutual assistance, or, by feats of Herculean strength, skill, and presence of mind, saving the lives of companions...

Mr. Willink was frequently applauded, and at the finish he was heartily thanked by the chairman, on behalf of the audience, for a lecture which while instructive, was certainly most entertaining.[143]

Over the succeeding years, Henry was called upon many times to lecture in a variety of locations on the theme of mountaineering – once under the title of "How not to Climb Mountains." His grandest venue was London's Royal Victoria Hall (now known as The Old Vic), where he lectured first in late 1890 and again in 1893. In each of the reports of his lectures he is celebrated as an entertaining and accomplished speaker, as well as an expert mountaineer and artist.[144]

In July 1890 Henry turned 39 years of age. He was a man of independent means having both wealth of his own and the money he had inherited from his father. He took the decision at this point to retire from his legal work, and to move his growing family out of central London to the country. The move was on doctors' advice, as it seems that their children were not thriving in London.[145] They may have considered other options, but decided that their move would be to Berkshire, just south-west of Reading, in the village of Burghfield. Their choice was influenced by its proximity to an old Callipers and Eton friend of Henry's, the Rev. William Osbert Clinton, who had been the Rector at nearby Padworth since 1888.[146]

"A Plunger"

An illustration by HGW

"Backing up"

An illustration by HGW

HGW wrote:
"The experienced mountaineer will find
shelter anywhere
(especially if his friend has a mackintosh)
Cader Idris
28 August 1877"

The Willink family in 1890

Henry and Mary, with Katie and George

Chapter 4

Highwoods

Incidence and reflection

ituated on Burghfield Hill, Highwoods has a magnificent view from the rear of the house to the east and south. In 1890 it was surrounded by 26 acres with stabling for up to eight horses, a coachhouse, kitchen gardens, park and woodland. It had been built just over twenty years before for Dr. Walter Bryant, who had engaged the well-known architect William Burn to create a house suitable for a gentleman of position.[147]

Dr. Bryant had purchased the land from Mr. James Taylor, of Culverlands, a major local landowner. Highwoods was then built for the doctor, his wife and three (adult and unmarried) daughters. They took up residence there in 1871.[148]

The house had a morning room, dining room, drawing room, library, kitchen, butler's pantry, housekeeper's room, offices, ten bedrooms and various dressing rooms.[149]

Dr. Bryant died in May 1888 and as a result the house came up for sale by auction on 30 July 1888. By November the following year it was in the possession of Mr. William Barningham, having been purchased for an undisclosed price, thought to be around £11,000 to £12,000.[150]

Highwoods, Burghfield, Berkshire,
from an old photograph

It was therefore probably from Mr. Barningham that Henry rented the property. The Willink family moved into Highwoods in August 1890.[151] On 14 February the following year their family was completed with the arrival of Francis Arthur Willink. He was baptised on 31 March at St. Mary's Church, Burghfield.[152]

Just before the family moved in, another book was published with Henry as illustrator. This time it was an adventure novel written by Clive Phillipps-Wolley with the striking title: *Snap – A Legend of the Lone Mountain*. Published in 1890 by Longmans, Green & Co., it had 13 illustrations by H. G. Willink. It was an adventure specifically written for boys and its reviews were unanimous in praising it. Below are two examples:

A better boy's story could hardly be desired. It begins with a cricket match, and ends with an extraordinary and perilous adventure in the Rocky Mountains. The interval is filled with a glorious succession of stories of Snap's career, which no boy can read without enthusiasm.[153]

The romance has avowedly been written for boys, and consequently a good deal of space is devoted to incidents that occurred in the hero's schooldays. The young paragon is then taken to the "Wild West," where he has a long series of victorious conflicts with wolves, panthers, bears and Red Indians. So exciting are his adventures that youthful minds cannot fail to be charmed by the recital of them. The tone of the book is exceptionally healthy. A more suitable gift to boys than this novel could not easily be obtained.[154]

What of the illustrations? In a lengthy review in *The Scots Magazine* it was with the illustrations to the book that the reviewer chose to start:

The illustrations themselves are enough to make the hair stand on end, and to produce that nerve-tingling which the sensation of height and danger gives to some people, and which, beginning at the toes, travels upwards through the whole body until it reaches the roots of the hair. Nothing can be better calculated to do this than the frontispiece of this book, entitled "In the Chimney," and one further on called "Snap's Sacrifice." [155]

The Willink family settled into Burghfield life. At the census in April 1891,[156] eleven people were living at Highwoods, with two visitors:

Henry G. Willink, 39, Barrister, living on own means
Mary G. Willink, 40
Catharine D. Willink, 5

"In the Chimney"

An illustration by HGW

"Snap's sacrifice"

An illustration by HGW

George O. W. Willink, 3
Francis A. Willink, 1 month

Then, 2 visitors:
Thos. Rolls Warrington, 39, Barrister, and his wife
Emma M. Warrington, 27

And six servants (all of course unmarried):
Frederick E. Cooper, 26, Butler
June Telford, 31, Cook
Alice L. Tattam, 27, Housemaid
Georgina Brown, 32, Nurse
Marie Perrier, 17, Nursemaid (born in Switzerland)
Alice Taylor, 17, Kitchenmaid

The family attended the local parish church - St. Mary's, Burghfield. At their arrival in 1890, the Rector was the Rev. Dallas Oldfield Harington.

Dallas Harington had been born in St. Peter Port, Guernsey, in 1832 or 1833. An Oxford graduate, he had previously served in four parishes and had a spell as Association Secretary for the Irish Church Mission Society before being appointed to the living in Burghfield in late 1879. He was to serve as Rector there until retiring in June 1911, by which time he was in his late seventies.[157]

The Rectory, opposite the Green in Burghfield, was large – 16 rooms according to the 1911 census – and therefore easily accommodated the Rector, his daughter Alice (aged 25 in 1890) and his father- and mother-in-law (Rev. Thomas and Mrs. Isabel Brock) and up to four servants. Sadly, Dallas's wife, Florence, had died in 1884.[158]

At the Willinks' first Christmas in Burghfield, Mary started as she meant to go on by entertaining 24 to tea from the Mothers' Meeting on Friday 26 December, and, on the next day, the Parish Room choir.[159] Henry and Mary also agreed to host the Burghfield & Sulhamstead Flower Show in "the beautiful grounds of Highwoods" in the summer of the following year.[160]

In April 1891, it was Henry's sad duty to act as executor for his brother, William Nicholls Willink, who had died in Farndon, Nottinghamshire. William's estate was worth just over £23,000, much of it being in trust for his son Thomas Wingfield Willink, who had lost both of his parents before his sixth birthday.[161]

Later Henry funded both an extension to St. Peter's Church, Farndon, and a brass plaque in memory of three members of his family who had connections with Farndon. The plaque read:

> To the glory of God and in memory of Sir George Nicholls K.C.B., Dame Harriet Nicholls his wife, daughter of Brough Maltby of Southwell, and William Nicholls Willink their grandson, all sometime resident in this parish. This north aisle was addad (sic) in 1893 by Henry George Willink during the incumbency of the Venerable Brough Maltby Archdeacon of Nottingham.[162]

May 1891 was an important month for Henry. He read his first paper to a Poor Law Conference and became one of the Bradfield Guardians of the Poor. I will delay consideration of these until the next chapter. Henry also began attending weekly meetings of the Sanitary Authority of Bradfield Union (which in the course of time became the Bradfield Rural District Council).

The Sanitary Authority of the Bradfield Union was chaired by Mr. Thomas Bland Garland of Hillfields. Born in 1819 in Trinity, Newfoundland, Bland Garland had spent much of his life in South America. He worked as a clerk and later manager for merchants Myers, Bland & Co. in Valparaiso, Chile – the Bland in the title being Thomas's uncle Horatio. Later Bland Garland installed the first apparatus to distill sea-water on a large scale, on the coast of Bolivia. Subsequently he became the Director of the Coquimbo Railway Company in Chile and was responsible for several extensions of railway along the west coast of South America, as well as other engineering projects – notably the cast-iron Mercado Central (Central Market) in Santiago, Chile, still a landmark in the city today.[163]

Bland Garland came to Burghfield in 1872 in response to his uncle Horatio's request. Horatio had left Chile in the 1840s and settled at Culverlands, Burghfield Common. He married the daughter, Emily, of the Rector of St. Mary's Church, Burghfield, the Rev. Henry Curtis Cherry. To anticipate the description of Hillfields, which figured so largely in the life of Henry Willink, Horatio Garland had Hillfields built in 1862. Horatio and Emily lived there happily until, on a journey to Jerusalem, Emily died and was buried in the Holy City in 1868.[164]

Following his wife's death, and since he had no heir, Horatio asked his nephew Thomas Bland Garland, his sister Arabella's son, to take that place. Horatio moved out of Hillfields to the "Bungalow" in the grounds, and gave Hillfields to Thomas as a life interest.[165] The "Bungalow" had three reception rooms, five bedrooms, and the usual kitchen, stabling, and more, all set in five acres.[166]

By 1892, therefore, Thomas Bland Garland had been involved in local affairs for 20 years. Highwoods, where Henry was living, is a short distance from Hillfields. Although many years Henry's senior, Bland Garland became a close colleague and friend of the newly arrived Willink. It was no doubt at Bland Garland's suggestion that Henry joined the Sanitary Authority of the Bradfield Union.

This committee met on Tuesdays almost every week of the year. Its role included planning decisions – the first meeting Henry attended, for example, on 19 May 1891 agreed "additions to the Firs" for General Hawley and "plans for a pair of semi-detached cottages for Mr. Jas. Dewe." [167]

Mr. Thomas Bland Garland

Drawing by HGW

As its name suggests, the Sanitary Authority also considered drains, water supply and health – for example monitoring and taking action over the frequent scarlet fever, typhoid fever or diphtheria outbreaks. It had a Highways committee (from 1895) that dealt with the state of footpaths, roads, bridges and electric lighting.

Henry attended meetings of the Sanitary Authority faithfully, being present for three quarters of the meetings in his first year (38 out of 51).[168]

Henry was, however, absent for the whole month of July 1891 on a very special trip to the Alps, to Zermaat in Switzerland, with his brother-in-law Ernest Carrington Ouvry, his great friend Clinton Thomas Dent, and his friend L. Mayne. This was a research trip, to collect material and drawings for a planned book, *Mountaineering* in the *Badminton Library* series. Mayne and Ouvry acted as models for Henry's illustrations, showing correct and incorrect methods in handhold, step-cutting, etc.[169]

69

Clinton Thomas Dent

By HGW, dated 28 July 1892

Henry, writing Clinton Dent's obituary in 1912, recalled this time:

> In the case of the Badminton book, he [Dent] persuaded me to go out and meet him in Switzerland, in 1891, on purpose to study and re-study everything on the spot. Every illustration was discussed and criticised, beforehand and in draft, many of them being inspired by him down to small details.[170]

The *Badminton Library* was a series of books on "Sports and Pastimes," which aimed to put into the hands of the inexperienced guidance by experts in the practice of these subjects. Previous volumes had included hunting, fishing, horse racing, shooting and football.

Mountaineering, by Clinton Dent with contributions by seven other individuals, was published in mid-1892, and was immediately well-received. The *Pall Mall Gazette* reported:

> We venture to prophesy that the new volume of the *Badminton Library* will have a great success. It deals exhaustively with one of the most fascinating of pastimes; it is written by famous experts; it is amusingly and profusely illustrated by Mr. Willink.[171]

The book begins with the early history of mountaineering and progresses through chapters on the principles of mountaineering, snowcraft, rock climbing and how to be properly equipped. It mainly considers Alpine climbing, but includes climbing in the Caucasus and hill-walking in the British Isles. Henry contributed a chapter on "Sketching for Climbers," giving advice on how to make and use sketches to enable the finding of best routes up and down a mountain. In total, Henry produced 10 plates and 92 smaller illustrations for the volume.

With his illustrations researched, Henry was back at Highwoods by 29 July to host the Burghfield and Sulhamstead Flower Show. Over the years ahead, the Willinks were to host this event frequently. This first occasion, unfortunately, was marred by rain for the greater part of the day.[172]

"Serve Him Right"

Illustration by HGW

"Crack
Climbers"

Illustration
by HGW

In October 1891, Henry gave a talk to parents of the children of the new – and free – Infant School, funded and donated to the parish by Mr. Benyon of Englefield. While the children were entertained by a Punch & Judy show, the parents listened to a series of speeches, including the one by Henry on the subject of Thrift. Since the parents no longer paid a penny for their child's schooling, Henry recommended that they invested those pennies until the children left school and then could benefit from the "nest egg" thus gained.[173] Henry was very keen on self-help as a means for the poor to improve their lot, as we shall see in the next chapter.

HGW
sketching

On 5 February 1892, Thomas Bland Garland died, aged 73, following a second attack of influenza, combined with jaundice. The *Reading Mercury* wrote "He was a thorough man of business, and most painstaking in everything he undertook, sparing no labour to master principles and details of every subject affecting the common good." [174] His funeral took place the following Wednesday (10 February), Henry being conveyed to St. Mary's Church in the fourth carriage with Henry Garland, a cousin of the deceased.[175]

In April that year, Henry was appointed Chairman, in succession to Thomas Bland Garland, both of the Sanitary Authority of the Bradfield Union and of the Board of Guardians of the Poor.[176] Henry had also just become more involved at St. Mary's Church, joining the School Committee, and being elected auditor for the parish together with the curate Rev. Hector Mawson.[177]

St. Mary's Church was at this time being restored. Works included a new chancel, new organ chamber and vestry, new stained-glass windows, new pulpit, new heating system and a complete re-building of the organ. Although not the major contributor to this work, Henry was one of four named as contributing towards the organ restoration, and one of the four who funded the heating of the nave. The restored church was reopened by the Lord Bishop of Oxford on 18 June 1892.[178]

Meanwhile, following Thomas Bland Garland's death, Hillfields came onto the market, to be sold by auction at the Queen's Hotel, Reading, on 15 July.[179] The advertisement by Messrs. Haslam & Son stated:

Freehold with Possession
"HILLFIELDS" BURGHFIELD HILL
NEAR READING

A charming country MANSION, containing conservatory entrance, three reception rooms, eleven bedrooms, bath-room, kitchens, and very complete offices, occupying a singularly choice position on the high ground above the village of Burghfield, with magnificent and very extensive views – stabling (six stalls and three loose boxes), coach-houses, farm buildings, entrance lodge, walled kitchen garden, glass houses, highly picturesque grounds, studded with choice conifers, rhododendrons and variegated shrubs, ornamentally timbered park lands, plantations and woods with an area of forty-five acres.[180]

More details of the property and its purchase will be given in Chapter 6. Here it will be sufficient to note that Henry and Mary bought Hillfields, and after eight months' extensive renovation works they took up residence there.

Almost certainly at this important time when Henry and Mary were completing their purchase of Hillfields, Henry was taken seriously ill. He had appendicitis, although at this date the procedures for diagnosing and dealing with it were not widely known. The term "appendectomy" was only coined six years earlier and the procedure was only known to relatively few by 1892.

Henry had the good luck to be being visited by Clinton

Dent, not only a great friend but also a renowned surgeon. Being a Fellow of the Royal College of Surgeons and Senior Surgeon at St. George's Hospital Medical School, London, Clinton Dent diagnosed appendicitis and lost no time, operating on Henry at his home, Highwoods, saving his life. Henry included this incident when he wrote the obituary of his friend in 1912:

> From one point of view, his [Dent's] salient characteristic was his thoroughness. This showed itself in all that he did where his interest was aroused, and he had an exceptional capacity for becoming interested in whatever he undertook.
>
> I have known him under many conditions. As a patient when he saved my life twenty years ago; and as father of a patient when, eighteen years afterwards, he performed a similar operation, happily at a less critical emergency, upon my son; as colleague on committees; as comrade upon the hillside; collaborating with him as illustrator of the *Badminton* book; playing cricket (indifferently), and golf (worse), with him, and bridge (sometimes to weariness), I never found his untiring thoroughness desert him.[181]

The Dent family and the Willink family became linked in 1920 through the marriage of Henry and Mary's niece Hester Clark (daughter of Mary's sister Harriet) and Clinton Dent's nephew Leonard Dent (son of Clinton's brother Edward). It was Leonard – Major L. M. E. Dent – who suggested that The Willink School should be named in honour of Henry (see page ix).

In December 1892 Henry became a Trustee of Reading Savings Bank.[182] Established in 1817 immediately following the first Savings Bank Act, Reading Savings Bank's offices were at 72 London Street – a building which to this day has the Bank's name in its brickwork, although now a doctors' surgery. The work of the Savings Bank was very much in line with Henry's views of the poor, which we will explore in the next chapter.

In an article discussing the effect of the 1817 Savings Bank Act, the benefits of these institutions were made clear:

> Savings banks… are admirably calculated, if properly directed, to encourage accumulation amongst the industrious classes… In addition to laying down rules and regulations for the government of the societies, and the security of the funds, a strong stimulus was held out by insuring the payment on a higher ratio than the average value of money, Government becoming bound to make good the difference from the public revenue.[183]

At the Annual Meeting of Reading Savings Bank in December 1892, at which Henry became a Trustee, the accounts showed that the Bank had 9,779 Depositors with an average investment of £28 16s 2d each.[184]

The Trustees of the Savings Bank gave their time voluntarily and their role was to oversee the running of the bank by the Committee of Management. Trustees were chosen because they were known to be upstanding members of the local community – landed gentry, clergy or aristocracy.[185]

While work to renovate Hillfields was continuing into 1893, Henry qualified as a justice of the peace for Berkshire.[186] With his professional background, Henry would of course have been an ideal candidate for being a J.P. His first duty was to be part of the Berkshire Quarter Sessions of the Peace held on Monday 3 April at the Reading Assize Courts.[187] Thereafter he often sat as one of the magistrates on the Reading County Bench on a Saturday, the first occasion being on 8 April.[188]

Altogether through the remainder of 1893, Henry was present for 18 of the 33 sessions reported in the *Reading Mercury*, which was about the same as the average attendance for the other justices of the peace. The Bench was chaired by either Captain Cobham or John Bligh Monck, being the more senior J.P.s.

As is the case now, a magistrate had to deal with a wide variety of types of offence. In his first few sittings, Henry had to consider: a defendant who had brought a herd of pigs into Berkshire without a licence; pub landlords accused of using incorrect weights and measures; poachers and trespassers; a man caught riding a bicycle without lights; parents neglecting to send children regularly to school; an inmate of Bradfield Workhouse who refused to work; drunken men guilty of disorderly behaviour at a public house; a man accused of shooting a dog; and perpetrators of various types of assault. A different slice of life from his usual experience, I expect.

The Willink family were able to move from Highwoods to Hillfields in September 1893, with the renovations complete. However, before we follow them we shall go back to Henry's London days to consider a most important thread in Henry's life – his involvement in the administration of the Poor Law.

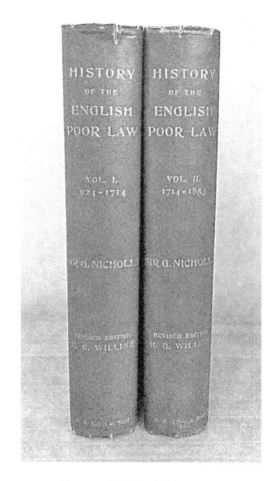

History of the English Poor Law
by Sir George Nicholls
Revised edition
Edited by HGW [189]

Sir George Nicholls, K.C.B.
Poor Law Commissioner
and Secretary to the Poor Law Board

– and also Henry's grandfather

Chapter 5

Guardian of the Poor

Hamlet iii, 1, 81.

rom the days when he was a young man, Henry had cared about the lot of the pauper in society. Perhaps this was not surprising, since his mother's father had been one of the three Poor Law Commissioners appointed in 1834 and had, in 1854, written the definitive history of the Poor Law in England since Saxon times.

Henry's first involvement in social welfare was when he was living in London before his move to Berkshire. He became interested in the work of the Charity Organization Society through contact with the Honorary Secretary, Charles (later Sir Charles) Loch.

The Society was both a co-ordinator of the work of other charitable societies and a leading voice in the quest to, as it saw it, stop the Poor Law creating dependency in those who could support themselves and to target those who were the most deserving. Henry's views entirely agreed with this approach, as we shall see. Henry became a member of the London Council of the Society.[190]

The first few articles that Henry wrote on issues relating to the relief of the poor were published in the *Charity Organization Review*, describing a system at work in the Netherlands. These were printed in 1889 in a 51-page booklet as *The Dutch Home Labour Colonies*.[191] One reviewer wrote:

> The writer considers that of the many experiments made in search of the best social system, none have been more interesting, or had a fairer trial, than that commenced in 1818 by the Society of Beneficence in the Netherlands, and still proceeding. The main idea was that pauperism could to a large extent be prevented by providing agricultural training and employment for able-bodied deserving destitute persons. Labour and beggar colonies were established, and seem to have flourished in Holland, but the author does not consider that it would be wise for our Poor Law authorities to establish or support, either in connection with our workhouses or otherwise, colonies like those of the Dutch.

There follows a sentence giving Henry's reasons for that conclusion, which sums up neatly his core belief about the relief of the poor:

> Not only are they expensive and not self-supporting, but it cannot, he says, be right, that he who comes to the State for aid should be placed by that aid in a better position than he who supports himself unaided.[192]

No doubt as a result of his involvement in the Charity Organization Society, Henry was elected in 1889 to be one of Paddington's Guardians of the Poor.[193] This was an important role, created by the Poor Law Amendment Act 1834. The Board of Guardians administered the workhouse of the Poor Law Union, which consisted of one or more parishes grouped voluntarily together. Henry remained a Paddington Guardian of the Poor until his move to Burghfield in August 1890.

In March 1891 Henry gave an address to the Lichfield Charity Organization Society Annual Meeting on the subject of "Charity," [194] followed in May by a paper at the West Midland Poor Law Conference on "The Function of the Poor Law in relation to Voluntary Effort." [195] In the first he defined charity as specifically not simply gifts of money, but "wise helpfulness personally exercised." In the second he contrasted the need to relieve destitution – the function of the workhouse – with other forms of distress that he believed should be treated by voluntary effort, not with Poor Law funds. In his paper, he continued:

> Poor Law relief, outside the workhouse, like most benefits that are received without personal contact between giver and receiver, constantly tends to create in the latter a feeling that it is received by right. The very thin distinction which, we are told by lawyers, exists between relief which a pauper has the right to demand, and relief which the State is under an obligation to give, has little meaning for him. It is enough that relief is practically a matter of certainty, and comes from no one in particular; for when the relieving officer comes in at the door gratitude flies out of the window. At any rate, this is the tendency, and the results are notorious. The more freely relief is given, the more it tends to grow, and the greater the demand for it. The recipient is not satisfied by it himself, and his neighbours are not satisfied that he should get it and not they. His children learn, while young, that dependence upon the rates is no disgrace; they become familiar with the idea of parish support, and the seeds of hereditary pauperism are sown in fruitful soil." [196]

It was a fortnight after this Conference that Henry joined both the Sanitary Authority of Bradfield Union and the Bradfield Guardians of the Poor. These two meetings were both held weekly on a Tuesday in the Board-room of the Bradfield Workhouse, with the former (as covered in the previous chapter) dealing with issues of planning, drainage, etc in the area, and the latter overseeing the running of Bradfield Workhouse (run on behalf of the Bradfield Union of 31 parishes) and the relief given throughout the area under the Poor Law.[197] Henry was to remain a Bradfield Guardian for 26 years.

Henry was elected to the Executive Committee of the

Reading Charity Organization Society and in January 1892 gave a talk at their annual meeting on "Old Age Poverty" with particular reference to possible legislation to award a pension to all over 65. Henry's view was that with thrift a young man should be able to purchase a deferred annuity for himself, effective from his 65th birthday, and so provide for himself rather than have the indiscriminate mechanism – rather like outdoor relief provision – from the Government.[198]

In April 1892, on the same day that he was elected Chairman of the Sanitary Authority of the Bradfield Union, Henry was elected Chairman of the Bradfield Guardians. The *Reading Mercury* reported that:

> At a largely attended meeting of the newly elected Guardians of the Bradfield Union held on Tuesday… it was proposed by Mr. Povey and seconded by Mr. Davies that Mr. G. H. (sic) Willink be appointed Chairman of the Board in succession to the late Mr. Thos. Bland Garland. Before the vote was taken Mr. Willink explained that he should (if elected) follow to the best of his ability in the steps of their late Chairman, Mr. Bland Garland, with regard to the administration of out relief which had proved of so much benefit to the poor as well as to the ratepayers of the Union, and he wished it to be clearly understood beforehand. The resolution was unanimously passed.[199]

Bradfield Guardians were already well known for their view on restricting outdoor relief to virtually nil. The distinction between indoor relief and outdoor relief is easily made. Indoor Relief was by means of the workhouse. The destitute were brought into the workhouse, fed and clothed, and put to work. Outdoor Relief was any Poor Law money given to anyone apart from the workhouse. It was a strongly held belief by the Charity Organization Society, by the Bradfield Guardians and by Henry himself, that Outdoor Relief led to a dependency upon hand outs and should be avoided. It was the role of the voluntary sector, they believed, to supply such relief as could be given without raising the pauper up to a level that was above his hard-working neighbour. In stating clearly before his election as Chairman that he would adhere to the same strategies as when his predecessor was in place, Henry was being consistent with beliefs he had previously expressed. The Board of the Bradfield Guardians was a model for many Boards around the country to show what could be done to reduce pauperism in the Union by this means.

Henry explained the Board's approach in a presentation to the Guardians of Leighton Buzzard Union in January 1893. It is worth hearing of the system he favoured at some length in his own words. The newspaper report of the meeting quoted Henry saying that:

> The Bradfield Board did not pay non-resident relief, because it was impossible to supervise the cases... In-doors [at the workhouse] no trouble was spared, and the few children they had to deal with were healthy. If he were asked how the result [of greatly reduced outdoor relief] he had given was brought about, his answer was that the end had been gradually attained. A few out-relief cases were at first cut off; but, as regarded the rest, notice was given that much relief would be discontinued, and people accommodated themselves to circumstances without being driven into the workhouse, as was shown by the figures he had given. He did not think that any hardship had been involved, and would not advocate a system of restricting out-relief if he did not think it was for the good of the poor, and from the conviction that it was best for them to be led to abandon the habit of relying upon relief from the rates, and to get rid of that family taint of pauperism which they found pervading most of those who came for relief... That the working of the system had contributed to bring out the quality of thrift was shown by increased membership in benefit societies and savings bank deposits. It had also resulted in bringing out a recognition of family ties and responsibilities, and more feeling and practical sympathy from neighbours.[200]

Henry continued to be in demand as a speaker at a variety of Poor Law Conferences, giving a major paper approximately every year. His next paper, in October 1893, was "The Local Government Bill, 1893, so far as it affects the administration of the Poor Laws," which he read to the South-Eastern and Metropolitan Poor Law Conferences.[201] This resulted in Henry being one of a delegation that went to 10 Downing Street to speak with the Prime Minister, Mr. Gladstone, in early November.

The delegation's concern was that the proposed Local Government Bill would have adverse affects on the administration of Poor Law relief through changes to the electorate, to the constitution of the local parish councils and, perhaps most importantly, to the rules of eligibility for being a Guardian.

Their views were summed up by Mr. Albert Pell, who said that "the Poor Law reformers of 1834 intended that the fund raised should be for the relief of destitution, and there was a fear lest it might be converted into a fund for giving bounties to the poor."

Mr. Gladstone, as was to be expected, gave a very diplomatic reply, appreciating that their "argument, as I understand it, is that the system of administering outdoor relief will be affected by the alteration in the constitution of the Board of Guardians." However, he stopped short of any assurances in the matter beyond saying that they had no intention of legislating on the matter of outdoor relief.[202]

I am sure that Henry and his fellow delegates would have been happy that they had been heard by the august Prime Minister, but probably left Downing Street less than satisfied with the final result. Henry was back in Burghfield in time to chair both the Bradfield Guardians meeting and the Sanitary Authority of the Bradfield Union meeting that day.[203]

Whatever Henry's fears may have been about the Local Government Bill (now the Local Government Act of 1894), he was elected the first chairman of the reconstituted Board of Guardians at the inaugural meeting on 1 January 1895.[204]

Henry continued to be very involved in the administration of the Poor Law both locally and nationally for most of the rest of his life. He was elected onto the committee of the South-Eastern Poor Law Conference in 1895, for example.[205]

Apart from his regular participation through papers to conferences,[206] Henry's remaining major contribution was to edit a new edition of *History of the English Poor Law* by Sir George Nicholls, his grandfather. This new edition was published in March 1898 and included a 78-page biography of Sir George Nicholls written by Henry.

Reviews were positive. The *London Daily News* wrote:

> No apology is needed for the appearance of this handsome new edition in two volumes of the late Sir George Nicholls' *History of the English Poor Law*. It has now been before the world for considerably more than forty years, and has long since taken its position as the standard authority on the subject of which it treats. This is, moreover, no mere reprint, for, besides Mr. Willink's interesting biography of the author prefixed to the first volume, it is to be followed before the close of the current year by the publication of a third volume, in which Mr. T. Mackay, who is well known by his writings on the subject of the English poor, will extend the inquiry from the point at which Nicholls left it down to these days.[207]

Hillfields

Chapter 6

Hillfields

 erkshire Record Office has the original *Sale by Auction* document for 15 July 1892, when the 68 Lots of the Hillfields estate were to be sold off "by direction of the Trustees of the late Horatio Bland, Esq, and of the late T. Bland Garland, Esq." [208]

Happily, the document has been annotated by hand to show who purchased which lot, and what the final price was. Lot One – bought by Henry for £9,000 – was the Hillfields house and main grounds:

Lot One.
The very attractive Freehold Property
KNOWN AS
"Hillfields," Burghfield Hill,
NEAR READING
Occupying a particularly healthy and desirable position on the high ground above the village of Burghfield and comprising:
A MODERN MANSION
Of pleasing appearance, very substantially constructed of grey and red bricks with stone dressings, conveniently arranged, very completely fitted, and containing:-
ON THE GROUND FLOOR – Conservatory Entrance, Hall 31ft by 9ft, with handsome pitch pine staircase, Library or

Morning Room, with a southern aspect, 17ft by 14ft, Drawing Room, 24ft by 21ft, inclusive of bay, Dining Room, 24ft by 17ft, Lavatory, Earth Closet, Butler's Pantry, Gun Room, Kitchen, Scullery, Servants' Hall, and two Store Rooms, with Servants Yard and Offices.

ON THE FIRST FLOOR – Central Landing, 17ft by 14ft, approached by the principal and a secondary staircase, Eight principal Bedchambers, sizes – 17ft by 14ft, 10ft by 9ft, 17ft by 15ft, 16ft 6in by 12ft, 20ft 6in by 17ft, 16ft by 13ft, 30ft by 8ft, and 14ft by 10ft 6in; Bath Room and Dressing Room with full-sized Bath, shower apparatus, and hot and cold water supplies, and a Tank Room, and

In the cool, dry and airy **BASEMENT** – Butler's Bedroom, secondary Servants' Hall, Lamp Room, large Wine and Beer Cellars, Dairy, Fruit Room, fitted Washing Room, with hot and cold supplies, &c., and a furnace room.

On the west of the Mansion is the enclosed Stable Yard with Stabling (erected in character with the Mansion), containing – Three Horse Boxes, Six Stalls, Washing House, Double Coachhouse, Boarded Harness Room, Groom's Room, Fodder Store and Lofts. Lean-to Chaisehouse and a two-bay Cart Shed, Brick-built earthhouse, Men's Closet, Cowhouse for six cows, Calf pen, Roothouse, enclosed and cemented Cow Yard with five-bay Cattle Shed, Concrete Fodder House with Granary over, Concrete Piggeries and capital Poultry Houses and Yards.

LARGE WALLED-IN KITCHEN GARDEN
With Vinery and Hothouse,
PITS, TOOLHOUSE, POTTING SHED AND GARDEN
BUILDINGS

The Pleasure Grounds
Are extensive, tastefully arranged, particularly charming, and studded with specimen Wellingtonea Gigantea, Aracaria, choice Conifers, Forest Trees, Rhododendrons, Roses and Flowering Shrubs.

The Park Lands
Are very ornamentally timbered and conveniently disposed.
There is a handsome LODGE at the main road entrance, and a
substantial BRICK-BUILT COTTAGE in the centre of the park
lands, with Piggeries and a Brick-built Turkey House.

The views from the Mansion and Grounds are extensive and very
charming, the sanitary arrangements are good, and the main
water supply is by iron pipes from the splendid water Reservoir,
shown on the plan on Lot 36, affording a constant and abundant
supply of good water.
This extremely desirable Residential Property has for many years
been in the occupation of the late T. BLAND GARLAND, Esq.,
and is in particularly nice order and condition. It occupies a
central position in a good Residential and Sporting locality, and
possesses attractive features not often found.
The total area of this Lot is 35a. 0r. 35p., and it will be sold with
possession.

****

For an additional £1,500 Henry bought Hillfields Farm
having 46 acres of arable and woodland, surrounding "A
Farmhouse, containing Two Sitting Rooms, 5 Bedrooms,
Kitchen, Scullery, and Offices, Wood and Coal Houses, Barn,
Granary, Stabling for 6 horses, Harness Room, Fodder and
Root Houses, Cowhouses, Lofts, Poultry Houses, Cattle and
Cart Sheds, and a range of concrete Piggeries, very
completely fitted." This land had various tenants in
occupation.

Finally, Henry also bought 12 acres of adjoining park land,
an orchard and some woodland.

As described in chapter 4, before the family moved from
Highwoods across the road to Hillfields, eight months of
extensive alterations were carried out. The family finally
moved into Hillfields in September 1893. The following
month:

On the 7th inst., the workmen, to the number of 50 who have been employed, were entertained to an excellent supper by Mr. Willink. The worthy host, who occupied the chair, expressed his entire satisfaction with the manner in which the whole of the work had been done. Mr. C. Mosdell responded, and on behalf of those present warmly thanked Mr. Willink for his hospitality. During the evening songs were sung by various members of the party, and a very enjoyable evening was brought to a close about 10.30.[209]

In January 1894, in spite of chairing both the Bradfield Guardians and the Sanitary Authority of the Bradfield Union every Tuesday, Henry spent a few days at Patterdale at the south end of Ullswater in the Lake District with his friend George Robert Jebb, Chief Engineer of the Birmingham Canal Navigations company. Henry later described what he called a "disagreeable surprise" on this trip:

We had been in British hills in winter often before, and Alps too. And we thought we knew something about them. But we found that sloping ground saturated with wet, then frozen hard as iron, and lightly dusted with powdery snow, might be distinctly queer going, even at gentle angles. Boot nails get no hold. Ice axes are no use. And if there are "drops" to go over – let alone precipices – at the foot of such slopes, well, really Nature is hardly playing fair. And I don't like to say what we failed to do! Of course, the same sort of conditions may occur wherever there are hills, humidity, and sufficient frost. To various degrees they certainly can be met with in suitable regions in the Alps before the sun has gained power. All I say is that it is humiliating to be beaten by Helvellyn! [210]

The following month, another volume of the *Badminton Library* was published, this time on *Big Game Shooting*, written by Clive Phillipps-Wolley with whom Henry had collaborated before when he illustrated *Snap: A Legend of the Lone Mountain* in 1890. On this occasion, Henry contributed just two illustrations.[211]

In July 1894 Henry attended the annual meeting of the local Oddfellows at Culverlands. In the previous two years he had hosted the meetings at Highwoods, although in 1892 he was "unavoidably absent" – he was on holiday in the Italian Alps from mid-July to early August at the time.[212]

The Oddfellows Friendly Society still exists today, boasting more than 280,000 members in 139 branches – one of which thrives in Burghfield. The purpose of Oddfellows is well described in an article written by Henry for the *Burghfield Parish Magazine* following a celebration of the centenary of the Independent Order of Oddfellows (Manchester Unity) in 1910. Henry wrote of the Burghfield "Loyal Star of the West" Lodge:

> The Lodge, which was established 17th October 1866, is one of the best in the Reading District, having, in December, 1909, 209 contributing members on the books, with an average age of 39 years, besides the nine honorary members. They show a total accumulated fund of £3039 15s 3d on 31st December 1909, during which year nearly £200 was paid in sick and funeral benefit and levies – total nett saving being nevertheless just over £158... The figures, good as they are, might be even better, and there are undoubtedly many lads and young men who ought to join the Lodge, which can be at 16. The advantages are great and obvious. Not only can an Oddfellow feel safe from some of the worst dangers of illness, which otherwise would deprive him of income at the time when he most needs it, but also he is a member of a vast and noble brotherhood, bonded together to maintain the welfare of each others' homes and families.[213]

Not needing to save money for such a "rainy day," Henry was one of the nine honorary members. He carried out the duties of the Honorary Treasurer of the Lodge from 1891 until retiring in November 1936.[214]

The size of the grounds at Hillfields not only allowed for such large community events as the Burghfield and Sulhamstead Cottagers' Horticultural Society Annual Show (for example, that of 1 August 1894) [215] but also enabled Henry to indulge in his passion for cricket on his own cricket pitch. Henry had been involved with Burghfield cricket from his arrival in the area and had, for example, presided over the celebration of the end of the 1893 season at a supper and "over the smoking concert which followed" at Highwoods. That season Burghfield had won all of its six club matches, but lost both matches against opposition brought in by Henry for "scratch matches." [216]

For one of these "scratch matches," Henry invited annually for August Bank Holiday Monday (then the first Monday in the month) a team from the Franklin Institute in London. Henry had been associated with this organisation in his Paddington days, from about 1886. The Franklin Institute, Henry wrote in an article in the *Burghfield Parish Magazine*:

> was opened 27th February 1875 in connection with the Sardinia Street Mission, Lincoln's Inn Fields, which was held in the house in which Benjamin Franklin once lived.
>
> It grew out of a suggestion made by some pupils in a night-school to Mr. E. C. Grey, who had been taking a class there, that some place might be found in which they might still occasionally meet, the school being about to be closed in consequence of the Education Act 1870.
>
> Beginning in an underground room, the Institute grew fast, and in two years the entire house had to be taken. In 1881 quarters were again changed to the present premises [in Betterton Street, Covent Garden]. The age of admission is from 14 to 16. Brothers and relations of old members have preference over other candidates. The subscription is 8s a year. There are classes in Arithmetic, Dictation, Writing, Geography, History, English Grammar, and French, and every member must attend at least one class a week…
>
> There is a Library, a Gymnasium, a Swimming Class, a Penny

Bank, a Benefit Club (duly registered), and a Football Club, besides the Cricket Club whose team we are so glad to welcome to Burghfield.[217]

The Franklin Institute's visit in August 1894 to play against Burghfield at Hillfields was remarkable enough for Henry to write a description for the *Reading Mercury*:

> We won the toss and went in first, on a rather wet wicket. The scores were, First Innings, Burghfield 34, Franklin's 86; second innings, Burghfield 47. The visitors thus won by an innings and five runs.
>
> There being still an hour and a half to spare, another match was begun between the same players. Franklin's went in first and lost six wickets for one run, the whole innings terminating for only 11. Burghfield made the necessary 12 for three wickets, playing out time with 25 for five wickets. Thus the side which won the first match by a whole innings were defeated by the same opponents (in a single innings match) by eight wickets.[218]

The other "scratch match" usually took place in early July with a similar visit from the Portman Club, Lisson Grove, London. This was a club for "working class lads" who came *en masse*, there being 59 visitors for example in 1895. They played a cricket match, and also enjoyed a hearty meal, before heading back to London by train from Theale.[219]

In the next few seasons, Henry played regularly for Burghfield Cricket Club, who from time to time used the pitch at Hillfields as its home. Some performances were notable – for example he was second highest scorer with 23 in an innings of 100 that defeated the Royal Berks Seed Establishment Cricket Club "A" Team in July 1895.[220] In fact, that season, Henry came second overall in the Burghfield team averages with a total of 67 in 6 innings (average 11.2) compared with J. Urlwin's average of 14.6.[221]

In the previous chapter, we saw that Henry had been elected the Chairman of the re-modelled Bradfield Guardians of the Poor on 1 January 1895 following the changes brought about by the Local Government Act 1894. At the same time, there were elections for the new Rural District Council of Bradfield (successor to the Sanitary Authority of the Bradfield Union) and a new Parish Council.

Henry had been chairing the Sanitary Authority since April 1892. For the new Rural District Council, there were four candidates for election for the two places for Burghfield. In a resounding success for the so-called Progressive Party, Francis Mattingley, a retired builder, and John Harding, a retired grocer, were elected, with local gentlemen Arthur Thursby of Culverlands and Henry George Willink of Hillfields being unsuccessful.[222]

That was not the end of the story, however, as at the first meeting of the Rural District Council on 1 January 1895:

> It was proposed by Mr. Harding and seconded by Mr. Mattingley that Mr. George Henry (sic) Willink be elected Chairman of the Council. Whereupon an amendment was moved by Mr. Dormer and seconded by Mr. Abery that the Chairman be elected from inside the Council and on the same being first put to the meeting it was lost by a large majority.
>
> The original proposition that Mr. H. G. Willink be Chairman of the Council was then put to the meeting and was carried by a large majority.[223]

Thus Henry, although unsuccessful in the election, was co-opted onto the Rural District Council as Chairman – at the recommendation of the two men who beat him in the election. As Chairman, Henry was also *ex officio* a member of the Finance Committee, Bye-Laws Committee and Highway Committee. A few days later, he was elected chairman of the new Parish Council too.[224]

In June 1896, another book was published with illustrations

by Henry – *Climbs in the New Zealand Alps* by E. A. Fitzgerald. Unsurprisingly, on this occasion, given the location depicted, Henry did not draw the illustrations from real life but from photographs. The book's publication was accompanied by an art exhibition of the photographs and illustrations at Clifford's Inn Hall, Fleet Street.[225]

In the previous year, Henry had illustrated an article by Clinton Dent on *The Alpine Distress Signal Scheme* in the *Badminton Magazine's* first issue. Both he and Mary had also contributed watercolour paintings to the annual Exhibition of the Newbury Art Society since its inauguration in 1892.[226]

Henry and Mary were becoming part of the County social scene, both locally and across a wider area. For example, whereas in 1895 they were invited as day guests to Lord and Lady Wantage's garden party at Lockinge House along with a few hundred others, by 1899 they were part of the much more exclusive house party of twenty-five.[227] In March 1897, Hillfields hosted the South Berks Hunt:

> On the 4th they met at Hillfields, Burghfield. A moderate field out, but oh, what a morning! I never remember to have been out for a day's hunting and had such a sample of weather. Rain, hail, wind, thunder, rainbows and friend Sol at short intervals. Mr. Willink provided us with something that was both grateful and comforting. Found a fox in the shrubberies below the house, running over the road at the bottom of the hill into some heavy plough at the back of the church, but could make nothing of it. Hounds found again in Clay Hill, running away nicely through Bulmoor away to Ufton Wood. We galloped through Ufton Wood, hounds running well to the accompaniment of thunder, lightning and bright sun varied by a rainbow and hailstorm, back by Ufton church, through Sulhamstead to Brickyard Cover and Bennet's Hill, where this fox beat us after a good 1½ hours.[228]

In June 1897 Henry and Mary were in royal company. The Royal Counties' Agricultural Show took place over the

Whitsun weekend in Prospect Park in Reading. On Bank Holiday Monday, Henry and Mary sat down to lunch at the Town Hall as part of a large group with His Royal Highness Prince Christian of Schleswig-Holstein, Queen Victoria's son-in-law and President of the Royal Counties' Agricultural Society, and his daughter Princess Victoria.[229] This was not the only time that Henry dined with His Royal Highness Prince Christian; two years later Henry attended a fundraising dinner for the Royal Berkshire Hospital, again at the Town Hall, which His Royal Highness attended.[230]

1897 was the year of Queen Victoria's Diamond Jubilee. Henry joined in the festivities in Burghfield, with over 400 children treated to a tea and about 700 adults eating a "meat tea" in two large marquees at Culverlands.[231]

Meanwhile, a more lasting Jubilee memorial was being built at Henry's instigation. The Old School, facing the Green in Burghfield, had recently become a Charity – of which Henry was Honorary Secretary – to be used as any or all of: Parish Room; a Working Men's Club and Reading Room; a place of meeting for any Religious or Friendly Society; the location for Lectures or Evening Classes or other event for the benefit of the inhabitants of the parish. To this room, Henry added a large room (36 feet by 16 feet) which was to be known as the Jubilee Room, a second and smaller room known as the committee room, and a covered and seated porch. Henry had the plans drawn up by his architect cousin, William Edward Willink, of Liverpool.

The official opening of the Jubilee Room was on 31 January 1898, when a supper was held in the room for the trustees of the Old School and the committee of the Working Men's Club. The key to the building was formally handed over to the Rector, Dallas Harington, as chairman of trustees:

> The Rev. D. O. Harington, after thanking Mr. Willink on behalf of the trustees and parishoners for his handsome gift, handed the

key to Mr. Claydon, chairman of the Working Men's Club committee, who, on behalf of that body, rehearsed his sincere thanks to Mr. Willink for his kind gift of the room. The Secretary read an address presented by the committee, to Mr. Willink, heartily thanking him for his gift. Mr. Willink having replied, other toasts were given, songs were sung, tunes on the handbells were rung, and a very enjoyable evening was spent.[232]

The first lecture at the Jubilee Room took place just two evenings later. It was the first of a series of four on Poultry Keeping given by Edward Brown F. L. S., under the auspices of the Berkshire County Council Technical Education Committee. Over 60 people attended.[233]

In the following year, Henry provided the money for a well to be sunk in order for the inhabitants of Kings Hill and Trash Green to have a better water supply. The following article appeared in the *Burghfield Parish Magazine*:

PUMP AT KINGS HILL

The water supply to this part of the parish has long been unsatisfactory in dry seasons; and during last autumn a "tube well" was sunk on the north side of the Burghfield-Theale road, at a point about 218 feet above sea level, and a pump fitted. The thickness of strata pierced were as follows, viz.: Top soil and London clay, 63 feet; basement beds of London clay, 17 feet; Reading beds, 68 feet, and the boring was continued 20 feet into the chalk, making a total depth of 168 feet. The work was carried out by Messrs. Callas, of Reading, at a total cost of £109 18s. 3d. (boring, tubes, and pump £97 1s.; fence, etc., £12 17s. 3d.). The spot selected, and the depth sunk, were as recommended by Mr. Blake, of H. M. Geological Survey, who says there will be an ample supply of good water, and whose forecast of the nature and thicknesses of the strata proved accurate within a foot or two. The pump can raise about 250 gallons an hour; and the more it is used the more freely the water will come. The supply is of excellent quality, and is absolutely safe against pollution.

If by the pump not being regularly worked the water is allowed to stand long in the pipes it may taste of iron, and the first few bucketsful should not be used. The expenses are being defrayed by subscription, the site being given by Mr. J. Herbert Benyon; and it is proposed to hand the whole thing over to the Bradfield Rural District Council, for the benefit of the public.[234]

A handwritten note by Henry in the margin of the Magazine states "I gave this except the site." The phrase "defrayed by subscription" in the *Parish Magazine* article seems to have been a device to cloak the giver with anonymity. The Bradfield Rural District Council duly took over ownership of and responsibility for the well and its upkeep.[235]

HGW entitled this 1898 photograph
Three Little Fairies, a "Princess" and a "Daisy"
The Fairies were (left to right)
Maisie & Hester Clark and Katie Willink.
"Princess" was the horse and "Daisy" the donkey

Hester and Maisie Clark were Katie's cousins – daughters of Katie's mother's sister Harriet (or Harry). The three girls were close in age – in 1898, Katie was 13, Hester 11 and Maisie 9. The Clarks were often at Hillfields, and the "three little fairies" were more like sisters than cousins. As we shall see, Hester and her husband Leonard Dent eventually owned Hillfields for many years.

In 1898 Henry was elected to the committee of the Royal Berkshire Friendly Society. The aims of this organisation were similar to both the Oddfellows and the Reading Savings Bank, both of which he had joined several years before. Henry remained on the Royal Berkshire Friendly Society committee, regularly attending the monthly meetings, until 1912 or 1913.[236]

Although Henry had been very active in the public sphere of the Poor Law administration and in social political matters, such as campaigning against the effect of the Local Government Act, he had not been party politically active. In his younger days, Henry had been a Liberal Unionist and follower of Gladstone. However, that had changed by the mid-1890s, when, for the 1895 election he supported Mr. W. G. Mount, the Conservative and Unionist candidate for South Berks.[237]

In 1900, thinking they were nearing the end of the Second Boer War, Lord Salisbury called what became known as the "khaki election" – named as such because it was an election in wartime. Mr. W. G. Mount had decided to retire from being a Member of Parliament, and so his son, Mr. W. A. Mount, became the local Conservative and Unionist candidate. At a meeting "in the Burghfield Schools" in September 1900, Henry gave the first reply to Mr. Mount's opening speech:

> Mr. WILLINK, in moving a vote of confidence in Her Majesty's Government and the candidate, referred to the services and the

devotion of Mr. Mount's honoured father, and remarked that Mr. W. A. Mount was a candidate whom they could all support heart and soul. It was most important that the Government should be returned with a still larger majority. (Applause.) ... he could not help saying that no Government could possibly have a better reason for dissolving than the present Government had. They were face-to-face with the re-construction of South Africa, with the reform of the Army, and with the enormous question of China. If the Government had committed the country to those things and then dissolved, the cry would have been that they should have consulted the people first. (Hear, hear.) ... Everybody knew the broad lines of Government policy, but the precise lines could not be laid down beforehand. The only honest thing to be done was to ask the country whom they would trust, and then leave the party chosen to do the best they could. He did not believe anybody knew what the Liberal party would do if they came into power – which they would not. He did not believe their so-called leaders knew themselves. (Hear, hear.) They hoped there would be no contest in South Berks, but that must by no means be taken for granted. If there was a contest it was the duty of every man to do the best he could to return Mr. Wm. Arthur Mount as Member for that Division. (Loud cheers and "We will.") [238]

From 1899 to 1901 Henry was the Vice President of the Alpine Club. He had first been elected to the Club in February 1880, a few months before his marriage, and had been on the Club's Committee from 1889 to 1892. He still enjoyed being among the alpine mountains – celebrating his 50th birthday in the Swiss Alps, for example, in July 1901 – but he also continued to seek gentler hills. In September 1900, Henry went up the Great Sugar Loaf Hill in County Wicklow in Ireland with his 12-year old son George.[239]

The Willink family at Hillfields about 1900

Henry, Katie, Mary, George and Francis

George was about to start his final year at St. Neot's School in Eversley in preparation for following in his father's footsteps at Eton. George went on to emulate his father as an Eton rower too. Francis also attended St. Neot's, three years behind George.[240]

Henry's daughter Katie was confirmed on Tuesday 18 February 1902 by the Bishop of Oxford at St. Mary's Church, Burghfield, one of 21 candidates from the parish. Two days later, the Willink family set off for Rome, with Katie taking her first communion there.[241]

Interior of Hillfields about 1901

Mary and her half-brother, Ernest Carrington Ouvry

Queen Victoria had died in January 1901 and was succeeded by her eldest son, Edward VII. The new King's coronation was held on 9 August 1902, and on that day Henry and Mary hosted at Hillfields a huge gathering from the parish to celebrate. Much of the afternoon was taken up with children's sports, with plenty of refreshments to keep everyone happy. The *Reading Mercury* reported:

> Fortunately, the weather kept fine, and nothing could exceed the kind welcome given by Mr. and Mrs. Willink and the members of their family to the 1,200 or 1,300 persons present. The

children especially had a happy time, being allowed free run of the lovely garden and grounds, and each receiving a Coronation box of chocolate....

During the evening the beautiful grounds in front of the house were lighted up by a large display of Chinese lanterns, while hundreds of fairy lamps surrounded the flower borders and terrace, and coloured lights were burnt, the whole effect being exceedingly pretty. Dancing was indulged in to the strains of Mr. F. Davis's Band. Shortly before 10 o'clock, a number of rockets were sent up by Mr. Willink and the National Anthem sung.[242]

The *Burghfield Parish Magazine* added that the "complete success of the festivities is largely due to the kindness and energy of Mr. and Mrs. Willink, who did all in their power to promote the enjoyment of all on that day." [243]

Hillfields, 1912
Left to right: Francis, Katie and Henry

Old Berkshire Shield

Design by HGW

Chapter 7

A Berkshire Alderman

Over it goes !

ne of Henry's passions in the latter half of his life was the development of local education. He had been interested in the work of schools since arriving in Burghfield in 1890, being elected onto the Parish School Committee as early as April 1892.[244]

In the 1890s there were three schools in the parish, all elementary (ie primary): the Burghfield National Schools, facing Burghfield village green, which had not yet moved to their current site further along Theale Road; Mrs. Bland's School at the end of School Lane, where Blands Court now stands; and Pingewood School which was situated just south of where the M4 now crosses the road below Kirton's Farm.

Henry and Mary frequently treated the school children from the various local schools, often at Hillfields. For example, in April 1898:

> … the children attending the Burghfield National Schools were kindly entertained to tea in the new schoolroom, by Mr. and Mrs. Willink. After partaking of a bountiful tea, the children marched to Hillfields, the residence of Mr. and Mrs. Willink, where various games were indulged in until dusk. Before breaking up, the prizes which were awarded for good conduct, regular attendance, general proficiency, &c., for the past year were handed to the recipients by Miss Willink.[245]

The organisation of education was significantly changed in the early 20th century, with School Boards being abolished and Local Education Authorities constituted to replace them following the 1902 Education Act. These LEAs were based on the county councils, and so Berkshire duly gained its Education Committee which first met on 6 June 1903.

Henry was recommended by members of Berkshire County Council to be a member of the Education Committee, being eligible as a Manager of an Elementary School.[246] At the first meeting of the Berkshire Education Committee he was also appointed onto the Elementary Education Sub-committee and the Bradfield RDC School Attendance Sub-committee. Subsequently he was also appointed onto the sub-committee to define the roles of the Education Committee and the organisation of its staff.[247]

The first few months of the Education Committee's work were very busy. For example, between the main meetings of 17 October and 5 December 1903, Henry attended at least 9 sub-committee meetings. The Elementary Education Sub-committee managed its work in Sections, of which Henry joined three. He chaired the School Management Section, which worked with teachers' representatives to set forth terms and conditions of service, and also to receive and respond to inspection reports. He was a member of the Buildings & Repair Section and of the Bye-Laws and School Attendance Section.[248]

As part of the Bye-Laws and School Attendance Section, Henry was involved in deciding how to encourage better attendance at the LEA's schools. The Section approved the idea of a medal to be awarded to all pupils of satisfactory conduct who had been neither absent nor late during the whole of a school year, and this was agreed by the Education Committee at its meeting on 21 January 1905.[249] Henry designed the medal, with the die being cut by Frank Bowcher, a noted maker of seals and medallions. The bronze medals were struck by the jewellers Mappin and Webb.[250]

The medal was circular with Berkshire Education Committee written around the outside. The obverse centre had Henry's design for the Berkshire Shield – a stag reaching up to an oak. On the reverse, the central design was "a group of children clustering affectionately around a woman, who may symbolize Education, or the Berks C.C. or some beloved school teacher," [251] surrounded by the words Never Absent, Never Late. The pupil's name was engraved into the edge. These medals were issued from 1905 until 1917.[252]

To the initial award of a medal for a year's perfect attendance was added a number of extensions for further years – clasps and ribbons, for example. For anyone completing seven years, a silver medal was awarded. In the report of the Berkshire Education Committee reviewing its first three years' work in April 1906, it details that 1,500 bronze medals had been awarded to that point.[253]

The medal shows that Henry's redesign of the Berkshire "badge" and flag was completed by 1904. Looking back in 1939 over fifty years of Berkshire County Council's history, the *Reading Mercury* quoted a memorandum presented at the County Council's meeting prepared by the Clerk (Mr. H. J. C. Neobard):

> The county badge of the stag and oak, as shown on the council's seal, appears to have been used by the council and the County Police on their official correspondence. Many years ago, the late Mr. H. G. Willink redesigned the county badge as it is now used, showing a naturalistic stag feeding with upturned head on the leaves of the growing branch of a tree, the whole being placed on a shield. Above the shield is a spray of oak and bay leaves surmounted by a royal crown, while beneath the shield is a scroll, with the word "Berkshire" written thereon.[254]

This design is pictured at the beginning of the chapter.

When Mr. J. Herbert Benyon stood down from being the

Chairman of the Education Committee in April 1908, Henry was chosen to succeed him and remained in that position until April 1932.[255]

In early 1905, Henry stood as a candidate for election to Berkshire County Council. As was the custom, he placed an advertisement in the local newspapers:

TO THE COUNTY COUNCIL ELECTORS OF THE
BURGHFIELD DIVISION OF THE COUNTY OF BERKS

Ladies & Gentlemen, Mr. Benyon having been co-opted an Alderman, I have been invited to come forward as a candidate for the Councillor's seat so vacated, and I trust that you will return me as your representative.

I am already not unacquainted with County business, and with those most actively concerned in it, through the work of the Rural District Council (of which I have been Chairman for more than ten years), and in other ways, particularly as a member of the County Education Committee since its formation, and should you do me the honour to Elect me, I am prepared similarly to give time and trouble as a County Councillor to the best of my ability.

In the matter of Education, one of the most important with which the Council have to deal, I am in favour of bringing up children in the way most likely to fit them for after-life, and of making it easy for those possessing the ability to carry on their training beyond the Elementary School, and to rise in the world. These things must cost money, but I fully recognise the importance of wise economy in this as in other departments, believing that those who are placed in a position of trust cannot be too careful to restrain the natural tendency of human nature to be liberal at the expense of others.

I am no stranger to you, and as a friend and neighbour of nearly 15 years' residence in the district, I hope I may rely on your support.

> Yours sincerely, HENRY GEORGE WILLINK
> Hillfields, Burghfield, Reading.
> 6th February 1905 [256]

There was one other candidate for the vacancy – Mr. Ernest Chance of The Poplars, Burghfield, a fellow Guardian of the Poor and District Councillor with Henry. The election date was 3 March 1905 and 672 out of 843 electors voted (although three spoiled their votes). The result was:

Mr. H. G. Willink	401
Mr. E. Chance	268
Majority	*133*

and so Henry duly became a Berkshire County Councillor.[257] He attended his first BCC meeting two weeks later, and was promptly made a member of the Public Health Committee, the Allotments & Small Holdings Committee and the Assessment & County Boundaries Committee.[258]

In October 1905, Henry stood down as Chairman of the Bradfield Board of Guardians, a role he had carried out since April 1892. The *Berkshire Chronicle* reported:

At the meeting of the [Bradfield] Board of Guardians, held on Tuesday, Mr. H. G. Willink tendered his resignation of the office of Chairman of the Board, and expressed his sorrow that he was unable, in consequence of increasing public duties, to continue the work of that office. In thanking the Guardians and officers for their loyal support, co-operation and assistance, he stated that he hoped the Board would continue to have at heart the best interests of the poor, as had ever been the case in the past, and that in carrying out the responsible duties reposed in them as a Board of Guardians, they would maintain the reputation gained of being one the best Boards in the country.

The Rev. A. J. P. Shepherd, in expressing the regret of the Board, moved the following resolution:- That this Board of Guardians has heard with great regret the announcement of the retirement of Mr. H. G. Willink. J.P., from its chair. They desire to record their appreciation of the unfailing courtesy with which, for 13½ years, he has conducted the business of the Board, and the untiring energy, conspicuous ability and zeal which he has

> brought to bear on all the details, both of indoor and outdoor relief, and the general work of the Board of Guardians. They trust his retirement will not mean the loss of his valuable services and help. The Board would add its thanks that Mr. Willink has, at their wish, so long postponed his resignation." [259]

Henry was co-opted at the next meeting back to the Bradfield Board of Guardians, as well as onto several sub-committees. He remained a Guardian of the Poor until April 1917, by which time he was a month short of completing 26 years on the Board.

In May 1905 Henry became, by virtue of a donation of £75 towards new buildings in London Road, a Life Governor of University College, Reading – the forerunner of Reading University.[260] The University had opened in September 1892 as an Extension College of Oxford University and was initially accommodated in the Hospitium in St. Laurence's Churchyard.[261] The College firstly expanded its site in the Valpy Street area of Reading, but by 1905 needed a new home on London Road.

In the following year, Henry was appointed by Berkshire County Council to represent them on the University College Council. He is listed as a Life Member of the University Court on the Royal Charter dated 17 March 1926 that changed the institution's status to the University of Reading. Henry became the Vice President of the Reading University Council from 1933 to 1937.[262]

In January 1907 Henry and Mary went with Katie (aged 21), George (18) and Francis (15) to the French Alps for a three-week holiday, in the area around Chamonix and Argentière. The family spent time skiing, walking and climbing, and of course sketching. Later that year Henry climbed his last Swiss mountain – Lo Besso (3667 m) – in the company of his son Francis.[263]

Celebrating Henry and Mary's
Silver Wedding Anniversary

"Henry George Willink
Mary Grace Ouvry
1880 Sept 9th 1905"

In bronze by Frank Bowcher (1864-1938)
6" by 4½" (15cm by 11cm)

In the following year, they did not need to go abroad to ski. In late April, there was a heavy fall of snow – about 18 inches (45 cm) deep – at Hillfields and so the family happily skied and tobogganed. Unfortunately, with the thaw came heavy flooding throughout the area for several days.[264]

HGW's sketch of his son George skiing

In 1909 Henry and Francis broke with tradition and instead of going on holiday in Europe they travelled to Jamaica and the USA. They sailed from Avonmouth on the RMS Port Royal for Kingston, Jamaica, departing on 3 April.[265] They stayed in Jamaica until 24 April, at which point they sailed on the SS Orinoco, arriving at New York five days later in the middle of a snow storm! [266]

HGW's sketch of their arrival in New York

Henry was elected to be churchwarden of St. Mary's Church, Burghfield, in April 1910,[267] replacing Mr. A. H. Thursby who had died in the previous June. He remained as warden until 1924.

At this Easter Vestry meeting, Henry was also re-appointed Honorary Secretary and Treasurer of the parish Bell Ringing society. This was a post he first took on in 1901 and carried out until 1913.[268] Although he did not ring the bells himself, in addition to ensuring their finances were well kept, he invited the bell ringers to Hillfields for an annual celebratory meal, usually in January or February.

It is worth listing the main responsibilities that Henry (at almost 60 years old) was undertaking at this time – that is, about 1910. The list below is not exhaustive as several roles required Henry to attend, and often to chair, a number of sub-committees. Henry's roles included:

- Berkshire County Councillor, and a member of its Standing & Finance Committee
- Representative of the Berkshire County Council on the County Councils' Association
- Chairman of Berkshire Education Committee and the Chairman or a member of many sub-committees
- Chairman of Bradfield Rural District Council and member of its sub-committees
- Bradfield Guardian of the Poor
- Justice of the Peace
- Member of the University College Council and Life Governor
- Churchwarden of St. Mary's Church, Burghfield, and with several other parish responsibilities including Trustee of various local charities and treasurer of several parish organisations
- Member of the Committee of the Burghfield Horticultural Society
- Vice President of Reading Charity Organization Society
- Trustee of the Royal Berkshire Friendly Society
- Honorary Treasurer of the Oddfellows Lodge
- Trustee of Reading Savings Bank
- Chairman of School Managers of Burghfield Schools
- President of Burghfield Cricket Club
- Vice chairman of Birmingham Canal Navigations

At the 1911 census, Hillfields had ten occupants: Henry and Mary, by now married for 30 years; Katie aged 25; George aged 23; and six servants – a cook, parlour maid, house maid, under house maid, kitchen maid and a house boy.[269] Francis (aged 20) was staying in London with his Aunt Harriet and Uncle Gerard Clark and two of his Clark cousins – Hester and Maisie.

Both George and Francis were at this time undergraduate students. George was nearing the end of his modern history degree at Corpus Christi College, Oxford, and Francis was in his first year at Brasenose College, Oxford – unlike his brother and father, not studying history but engineering. After graduating, George entered the Inner Temple in London as a Barrister, being called to the Bar in 1913.

In August 1912, Henry's close friend Clinton Dent died after a short illness which seems to have started with his catching a chill when getting wet playing cricket. He then developed symptoms of blood poisoning and had intensive medical care for a fortnight, but died following a few days of semi-consciousness. He was 61 years old.

Within a few days, Henry had written a memorial of his friend for the *Alpine Journal*. They had been at Eton together, although in different houses, and had often been climbing and walking together in the years since. Henry owed Clinton the debt of his life with the appendectomy he performed in the summer of 1892 on a table at Highwoods (see page 76). Henry concluded his memorial to his friend with this paragraph:

> But what we loved most in him was not his physical characteristics, and what we most looked up to was not his artistic or intellectual qualities. It was something indescribable in the man himself: his sympathetic insight; his extraordinary power, so well used, of inspiring confidence; and, chief of all, his reserved warm heart, which irresistibly drew out affection to meet affection – there were the sources of the influence we felt to be one of the best parts of our own lives.[270]

Just before Clinton Dent's death, Henry had been on holiday in Scarborough and Whitby, and then on some western Scottish Isles. By the end of the first week in September the family were off again, this time to Galway in Ireland, returning at the end of the month. On 17 October, they were in Liverpool to wave goodbye to Katie and George, who sailed for Colombo, Ceylon (now Sri Lanka), in the SS Worcestershire.[271]

On 8 February 1913, Henry received the honour of being elected as an Alderman of Berkshire County Council. At the normal quarterly meeting of the Council at the Assize Courts in Reading:

> The first business was to elect an Alderman in the place of Capt. A. W. Cobham, resigned, and voting was taken by papers.
>
> Colonel G. C. Ricardo and Mr. H. G. Willink had been nominated, and the voting resulted in the election of the latter gentleman, who received 21 votes against 19 cast for Colonel Ricardo.
>
> Mr. WILLINK: I thank the Council for the honour they have done me. We have had a very good race.
>
> Col. RICARDO: A capital race (Laughter).[272]

Berkshire County Council had, at the time, a Chairman, Vice Chairman, 10 Aldermen and over 40 Councillors. Being elected by his peers as an Alderman conveyed a recognition of Henry's status within the Council, that he was highly thought of and considered an effective and valuable member of the Council. Henry remained an Alderman of Berkshire County Council until his death in 1938, and thus could style himself Ald. Willink for the last 25 years of his life.

Soon after becoming an Alderman, Henry and Mary enjoyed a month's break. They started with a cruise, First Class on the SS Morea to Marseilles via Gibraltar and Port St. Vincent, leaving London on 4 April 1913. They stayed a few days in Hyères on the French Mediterranean coast and then went on by train to Bellagio on Lake Como in Italy. Along the way, probably at Hyères, they were joined by Katie.[273]

HGW's sketch of the country near Hyères, France

The original is a watercolour

Marriage of Catharine Dorothy Willink
and Edward Fielden Pilkington
(Katie and Ned)

28 January 1914

Chapter 8

The War Years

Topographers

ary and Henry's daughter, Katie, was the first to leave the parental nest. On 28 January 1914 Katie married Edward Fielden Pilkington (known as Ned) at St. Mary's Church, Burghfield.

The Willink family and the Pilkingtons knew each other well through mountaineering. Ned's father, Charles Pilkington, was a close friend of Henry's and was one of the contributors to the *Badminton Library Mountaineering* book in 1892. Charles wrote two of the fifteen chapters – "Climbing without guides" and "Hill climbing in the British Isles." Charles had also been President of the Alpine Club from 1896 to 1898. While being closely related to the Pilkingtons of Pilkington Glass fame, Charles was a Director of Pilkington Tiles and of Clifton & Kersley Colliery near Manchester. His son Ned followed in his footsteps with both roles, as Director of the Tile Works from 1914 and of the Colliery from 1917.[274]

Katie and Ned's marriage was reported at some length in the local newspaper:

Wednesday last was a day long to be remembered in Burghfield, and at the Parish Church, which was the day and place of the wedding of Miss Catharine Dorothy Willink, only daughter of Mr. and Mrs. H. G. Willink of Hillfields, and Mr. Edward Fielden Pilkington, son of Mr. and Mrs. Pilkington of The

Headlands, Prestwich, Manchester. The bride is very popular in the parish, having endeared herself to all in various ways, among others as a district visitor, and also as conductor of the local choral society, who have for several seasons given most excellent concerts, and the greatest interest was manifested in the wedding. The time of the ceremony was fixed for 2.15pm, previous to which time the organist, Mr. T. J. Bennet, played appropriate music. The marriage service was performed by the Rev. J. D. Ouvry, Vicar of Grazeley and uncle of the bride. The Rev. W. H. George, rector of the parish, read the prayers and the address from the altar was impressively given by the Rev. Canon J. Wakefield Willink, Rector of Birmingham (the bride's cousin).[275]

After the ceremony, there was a reception at Hillfields. The church bells continued to be rung in celebration at intervals throughout the day and the children of the local schools were given a half day's holiday! The next day, the happy couple headed for Italy for their honeymoon.

Soon afterwards, Henry and Mary embarked on their first "motor tour" in their new car. They travelled through Gloucestershire and down into Cornwall.

In March 1914, Henry offered a field he owned in Burghfield Common to the Parish Council for use as a Recreation Ground. The Council accepted "the generous offer of Mr. Willink of this great boon to the parish." [276] The conveyance of the land was completed on 30 September 1914, and the Recreation Ground, near what is now the site of The Willink School, has been a great resource for the local community ever since.

By the time the land was conveyed, everyone had rather more than recreation grounds on their minds. When war was declared on 4 August 1914, both of Henry and Mary's sons were mobilised as they were already members of branches of the Army.

Henry and Mary Willink on their "motor tour"
February 1914

The motor car was a 1913 Fiat Tipo Zero Torpedo,
which had a 1.8 litre engine and a 40-mph cruising speed.
It managed just under 20 miles per gallon of petrol.

LK 4987 was a late 1913 registration
by London County Council [277]

George was a Second Lieutenant in the Inns of Court Officers Training Corps. Francis, who had graduated that summer from Brasenose College, Oxford, with a second-class degree in the science of engineering, was a Lieutenant in the Territorial Force, 4th Battalion, Princess Charlotte of Wales's, Royal Berkshire Regiment.[278]

Henry chaired two public meetings in Burghfield to explain the causes of the war and to encourage young men to join up for Kitchener's Army – at the Technical School on 18 August and at the Jubilee Room the following evening. At St. Mary's Church the Sunday sermon was preached on the text "Shall your brethren go to war and shall ye sit here?" from Numbers 32:6.[279]

Henry did not simply encourage others to join up. Being 63 years old, however, he was only able to be a part of the National Reserve. By September 1914, he had become Captain, Commanding the No. 8 Company of the 1st Battalion, Berkshire National Reserve.[280]

Despite the war, 1914 ended on a high note for the Willink family – Henry and Mary's first grandchild was born, at Hillfields on 17 December. Katie and Ned became proud parents of daughter Noel Mary Pilkington.[281] From a very early age, Noel called her grandfather "Ba," and the name stuck from then on in the family. Possibly by a kind of association, to the next generation the family nurse, Georgina Brown, became known as "Na" and Francis was "Uncle Fa."

In common with many parishes, Burghfield took in families of Belgian refugees. The Laurent family (father, mother and two daughters) from Louvain, where their house had been burnt to the ground, were accommodated at the Old School in Burghfield, arriving there on 24 October 1914. Another family of four moved into "Barnhey" in Burghfield Common. The Willinks were closely involved in caring for both families, co-ordinating local charitable gifts with Henry being Hon. Treasurer of the funds donated.[282]

Noel - Ba

A photograph from May 1917,
with names written below by HGW, aka Ba

As well as his continuing work as an Alderman on
Berkshire County Council, chairing the Berkshire Education
Committee and Bradfield Rural District Council, and the very
many other roles he took, Henry wanted to work for the war
effort. In the early days of the war he was closely involved in

125

recruiting for the Police Special Reserve.[283] He was a member of the Berkshire War Agricultural Committee from its inception [284] and from August 1914 he was a member of the Berkshire Committee of the National Relief Fund.[285]

With the onset of conscription, councils – including the Bradfield Rural District Council that Henry chaired – had to create tribunals. These were to hear cases of men who claimed they were disqualified on grounds of conscientious objection, poor health or "starred" occupations. These last were those areas of work considered vital for the war effort. Henry chaired the Bradfield District Tribunal throughout the war from April 1916, often weekly.[286] This must have been a difficult job, and potentially an unpopular one.

With all the war work that Henry had taken on, in addition to his normal load, he was now on at least 45 committees or Boards,[287] several of which he chaired. By the autumn of 1916 he was exhausted and became seriously ill. He took to his bed on Wednesday 11 October and was unable to return to his usual duties until the very end of the year. At much the same time, Mary also became ill and needed several weeks of bed rest and, as we shall see, never really recovered.[288] Henry, however, was on the road to recovery when their daughter Katie gave birth to their second granddaughter, Honor Brocklehurst Pilkington on 4 December 1916, at Hillfields.[289]

Although Henry did resume his busy schedule in January 1917, medical advice to him was to reduce his responsibilities otherwise he could expect to become seriously ill again. He therefore decided that, at the next annual meetings of both the Bradfield Rural District Council and the Bradfield Board of Guardians of the Poor, he would resign. This reduced his committee load by two main committees and 14 sub-committees.

Henry had been a member since 1891 of both the Board of Guardians and the Sanitary Authority (which was replaced by the Rural District Council in 1894). He became chairman of both bodies in 1892, resigning as chairman of the Board in 1906 although he continued being a member.

Both the Council and the Board paid marked tribute to Henry. The Rev. Alfred J. P. Shepherd, Chairman of the Board of Guardians, said:

> Mr. Willink's long tenure of office was remarkable for the ability of his administration, the patience and care with which he directed the business of the two authorities upon the soundest principles, and the courtesy, kindness and tact, which won the affection and esteem of his colleagues.

He then moved the following resolution:

> "The Board and Council desire to record the value they place upon the services Mr. H. G. Willink has unstintingly rendered to them during the years he has been a Guardian and a Councillor.
>
> "They remember his unerring courtesy and tact during his Chairmanship of the Board of Guardians (1892 – 1906), of the Rural District Council (1894 – 1917) and of their numerous Committees, his unfailing energy in the work and conduct of the Committee, and his readiness at all times to take responsibility and make decisions.
>
> "They regard the unanimity and the success of the developments of the past years as a result of his patient determination to ensure that each action of the Board and Council should be the action of all its members, and not of a voting majority, and they will not forget that he always presented a wide outlook for the amelioration of poverty and suffering, not merely by the immediate relief of the sufferer, but by attacking and removing the cause." [290]

It was not long before Bradfield Rural District Council lured Henry back, but this time just onto their Food Economy Sub-committee, in May 1917.

Henry and Mary's sons fought for King and Country. Their younger son, Francis, was the first to see action. He and his regiment, the 1ˢᵗ/4ᵗʰ Battalion Royal Berks, went to France at the end of March 1915. The photograph of Francis on the opposite page shows him on 30 March, on the point of departure for the Front. In September 1915, he was invalided back to the UK. He had been promoted from Lieutenant to temporary Captain on 16 September 1914, and on 19 April 1916 the rank was made permanent.[291]

Meanwhile, his brother George also became a temporary Captain on 31 July 1915.[292] At this point, Henry and his two sons were all ranked as Captains. In the June of the following year, George was transferred from the Inns of Court Officer Training Corps to the 2ⁿᵈ/4ᵗʰ Battalion Royal Berkshire Regiment and he and his Battalion went to the Front in July 1916. His Captaincy became permanent on 17 November 1916.[293]

Back in Burghfield the Parish Magazine was not published for six months in 1917 as there was no-one to produce and edit it. Henry and Mary decided to take the job on, and in the first issue (October 1917) must have been extremely proud to be able to give some special news about George:

> Captain G. O. W. Willink was Mentioned in Despatches in May and has just been awarded the Military Cross for distinguished conduct in August. He has commanded "A" Coy. in the 2/4 R. Berks Regt. since it went out in July 1916, and has seen service in many parts of the line in France and Flanders.[294]

In the same edition, it was noted that "Capt. F. A. Willink is at present invalided to the Reserve."

Details concerning the M.C. emerged during October. The *Reading Mercury,* under the headline CAPTAIN WILLINK'S BRAVERY," stated:

Capt. F. A. Willink

1/4 Battalion
Royal Berks
Regiment

March 1915

(Territorial Army,
Infantry)

Capt. G. O. W.
Willink

2/4 Battalion
Royal Berks
Regiment

July 1917

(Territorial Army,
Infantry)

> The Military Cross has been awarded to Captain G. O. W.
> Willink, Royal Berks Regiment, son of Mr. H. G. Willink, J.P.,
> of Burghfield. A number of gunners belonging to the Royal
> Horse Artillery were buried during a German bombardment
> which preceded a British attack on the enemy. Captain Willink
> went out, in spite of the heavy fire, and personally assisted to dig
> them out, doing splendid work. He had some marvellous
> escapes, his steel helmet being dented by a piece of shell. The
> major of the battery saw the affair, and insisted on having the
> names of those who had shown such pluck. Captain Willink is a
> fine soldier and extremely popular in his battalion.[295]

George received his M.C. from King George V at
Buckingham Palace on 7 November 1917, returning to the
Front soon after.[296]

Meanwhile, at Hillfields, Mary did not recover her health
after taking to her bed in October 1916. She would often be
carried, in her bed or chair, outside on fine days to enjoy the
gardens at Hillfields. Henry and Mary went away to Canford
Cliffs Hotel, Bournemouth, for "17 happy days" in
September/October 1917.[297] When George was home on
leave to receive his M.C., the photograph on the page opposite
was taken – the last photograph taken of Mary.

Mary died peacefully on Sunday 10 February 1918 aged
67. The death certificate identified the cause as "Progressive
Pernicious Anaemia." [298] Her funeral was at St. Mary's
Church, Burghfield, on the following Thursday. The *Reading
Mercury* reported that the "church was crowded with a
sympathetic congregation, and a large number were unable to
obtain admission." As well as the local gentry, it was notable
that "the house and outdoor servants, and others from all the
principal houses in the neighbourhood" were there to pay their
respects. The report called Mary "one who would be sorely
missed for a very long time in the parish and neighbourhood."
Unfortunately, George was unable to travel back from France
for the funeral.[299]

Standing, left to right: Henry, Francis, George
Seated: Mary

November 1917

The *Burghfield Parish Magazine* printed a letter from a friend, who wrote the following of Mary. The key word both from this letter and from the memorial opposite is "happy" – a good quality to be remembered for!

There never was one whose life was more spent in trying to make others happy. She joined in their pleasures, whether they were young or old, she sympathised with their troubles, and she had a kind word for those who were in fault or blamed. She thought evil of no-one, and all who came within her sphere of influence were better for it. The longer one had known Mrs. Willink, the more difficult it was to take count of the loss to oneself and one's friends…

She had the gift of inspiring happiness, and that sprang from her loving sympathy with all that is good. Her joy in all that was beautiful in nature, for she was an artist and had an artist's eye; her appreciation for what was sound in literature, for her taste was very true, as those who joined her Shakespeare readings knew; her pleasure in good music; all these showed how many-sided her interests were; and that her exquisite tact and judgment were guided by a soul that sought out what was good and beautiful.

Nothing was more beautiful in her life than the way in which she shared in her husband's work, and took an interest in every act of her children. They were ever in her thoughts, and yet she could think of others too, and be the best friend of all who were fortunate enough to know her. In grateful memory, we all thank God for having given us the happiness of knowing our dear friend Mrs. Willink, and having found in her one who has left those she knew better for her example.[300]

The marble tablet opposite was erected early in 1919 following a Faculty granted by the Diocese of Oxford.[301] A similar tablet was erected in memory of Mary in Wing Church, Buckinghamshire, the parish where she had spent the first 30 years of her life.

SACRED TO THE DEAR MEMORY
OF

MARY GRACE WILLINK

DAUGHTER OF THE LATE REVᴰ P.T. OUVRY VICAR OF WING BUCKS
AND WIFE OF HENRY GEORGE WILLINK OF HILLFIELDS
SHE WAS BORN 20 JULY 1850 AT WING VICARAGE
AND WAS MARRIED 9 SEPT. 1880 IN WING CHURCH
SHE DIED 10 FEB. 1918 AT HILLFIELDS
AFTER A HAPPY LIFE
LOVING AND BELOVED
THE LAST 27 YEARS BEING SPENT IN THIS PARISH
IN WHOSE QUIET CHURCHYARD SHE WAS BURIED
ON 14 FEB. 1918

Mary's Memorial
on the north wall of St. Mary's Church, Burghfield

Henry's sorrow was about to be doubled. He received a "field card" from George in France, dated 27 March 1918, saying that he was quite well and that he hoped that the battalion had got through the worst. On 5 April, Henry was officially informed that George was "missing, believed killed" on 28 March.[302] There followed a terrible period of uncertainty, with dwindling hope. It was not until three weeks later that it was confirmed that George had been killed in action.[303]

George, leading his battalion from the front, had been shot through the head in a "gallant counter-attack" near the French village of Lamotte-en-Santerre. Orders had come to them to advance at noon, but there was no artillery barrage to support them and very little cover, while the enemy swept the area with machine gun fire. Unsurprisingly, losses were heavy that day.[304]

His Brigadier said of him: "The more I saw of him, the greater grew my respect and affection for him… He was a real rock, strong, capable, self-reliant, and possessed the complete confidence of every man in the battalion." The *Reading Mercury* added that "Many will confirm this and much more, for he loved peace, not war, and was a devoted son, brother and friend, with hidden depths of noble character." [305]

Captain George Ouvry William Willink, M.C., MiD, was buried in Villers-Bretonneux Cemetery, Somme, France.[306] He was aged 30 when he died.

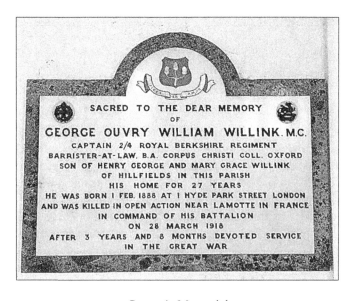

George's Memorial
on the north wall of St. Mary's Church, Burghfield

Meanwhile, in June 1918 the *Burghfield Parish Magazine* told Francis's war story:

> Condolences with Capt. Francis Willink, who, sorely against his will, is, after fifteen medical boards, gazetted out of the Army "on account of ill-health contracted on active service" … He joined the 4th R. Berks and was a Lieut. when war broke out, soon afterwards being made a Captain and given command of "E" (the Newbury) Coy. In March 1915, he went to France with the Battalion, which had become the 1/4th upon the formation of the 2nd unit. They went immediately into trenches at "Plug Street," afterwards holding sections of the line by Bethune, and later Hebuterne. The trying conditions of active service, however, told upon him and brought on dysentery and colitis, and after holding out as long as he could, perhaps too long, he was invalided home in September 1915. Since then he has done a lot of useful work with the 3rd line at Weston-super-Mare, and Windmill Hill on Salisbury Plain, and for some time was Draft Officer. But his health did not really improve and a year ago he was transferred to the Reserve, since which time he has been twice medically examined and is now declared unfit for military service. He has given his health, as his brother has given his life. Fortunately, there is still useful work open to him to do of national importance.[307]

The announcement was duly made in the *London Gazette* that "Capt. F. A. Willink relinquishes his command on account of ill-health contracted on active service, and is granted the hon. rank of Capt. 1st June 1918." [308] Francis was entered on the Silver War Badge Roll in July. The Badge was a small circular sterling silver badge inscribed "For King and Empire" and "Services Rendered." It was both an honour, like a medal, and a symbol that the owner had done their duty and was not in civilian clothes because they were too cowardly to sign up.

The Armistice was signed on Monday 11 November 1918 and was celebrated in Burghfield with "the ringing of house bells, the hoisting of flags at well nigh every house, and merry peals of church bells." The following evening a thanksgiving service was held at St. Mary's Church.[309]

Following the Great War things would never be the same again for the country or for Henry. His was now a much lonelier life; just Francis still lived with him at Hillfields. Henry took great delight in Katie's children, Noel and Honor, but they lived near Manchester and so were only occasional visitors.

Ba and Honor
1918

Henry was also supported by his sister-in-law, Mary's sister, Harriet, known as Harry. The families (Henry and Mary Willink and Harry and Gerard Clark) had always been close and frequently visited each other. Following Mary's death, Harry and Henry wrote to each other almost daily.

As well as memorial tablets on the wall at St. Mary's Church, Henry arranged for Mary's grave to be suitably marked. Since George was not buried in Burghfield, Henry decided that the memorial should remember him too. George is therefore remembered on the reverse side of the grey Cornish granite cross that marks Mary's grave:

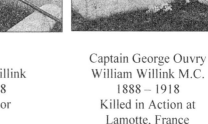

Mary Grace Willink
1850 – 1918
Fides et Amor

Captain George Ouvry
William Willink M.C.
1888 – 1918
Killed in Action at
Lamotte, France

In May 1919, there was a meeting, called by Mr. Job Lousley, Chairman of the Parish Council, at the New Schools in Burghfield to discuss the question of a memorial of the part Burghfield had played in the war. A committee was formed and recommended several actions. The major memorial was to be the erection of a cross in the churchyard with the names of the 39 local men who had been killed. The committee also recommended that the two recreation grounds should be improved by the laying down of a cricket pitch on each. Lastly, it was suggested that there should be a Peace Celebration.

The Peace Celebration was held on Saturday 26 July 1919. The children from the various schools in the parish marched to the church with flags and banners in time for a short service at 2.15pm. Then with demobilised soldiers and sailors at the front, all marched to the lower field at Hillfields for the main event. Children played various sports, and there was a tea for all. At the conclusion, "Mr. Willink, in a brief address, thanked the men for the part they had played in the war, and sympathetically referred to those others who had made the supreme sacrifice." The Burghfield Brass Band played throughout the day, which ended with a display of fireworks.[310]

The War Memorial Cross had its Service and Dedication over a year later, on Sunday 14 November 1920. The ex-service men gathered on Burghfield Common and marched down the hill to the church, where the bells tolled half-muffled peals. The church was overflowing for the 3pm service.

Both readings from the Bible (Wisdom 3:1-6 and I Thessalonians 4:13-18) were read by Henry. After hymns and prayers, the Lord Lieutenant of Berkshire, Mr. J. Herbert Benyon, led the way outside to the Memorial Cross. There, he loosened the ropes that held the Union Flags that covered the Cross. The Rector pronounced the Dedication, reading out the names of the men commemorated. Two buglers of the Royal Berkshire Regiment sounded the "Last Post" and "Reveille," followed by the assembled congregation singing the National Anthem.

The Cross stands 14ft 6in (4.42 metres) tall and is made of Portland Stone. The design – a cross with shaft and arms of octagonal section, rising from an octagonal base and steps, and bearing on its face a bronze cross-hilted sword – was by Sir Reginald Blomfield R.A. and it was constructed by Messrs. H. T. Jenkins & Son, Torquay. It was erected by Messrs. H. D. Higgs & Son of Burghfield. Around the upper part of the base of the cross the names of the fallen are engraved, including "G. O. W Willink. Capt M.C." [311]

Dedication of the Burghfield War Memorial Cross
14 November 1920

Henry is standing on the right of the photograph

Henry in July 1921
Photograph taken on Breukelen Broads, Netherlands

Aged 70 years and 1 day!

Chapter 9

Twilight

A mountain arab

harles George Willink Pilkington, Henry's third grandchild, was born in early 1921. Unlike his sisters, Noel and Honor, Charles was born in Lancashire, at Ned and Katie's home, Ingleside, outside Manchester.[312]

The 1920s saw many additions to the next generation in Henry's extended family. As well as his grandchildren – a fourth, Edward Michael Pilkington (known as Michael), was added in Spring 1924 [313] – there were great nephews and nieces. The favourites were the five children of Harriet and Gerard Clark's daughter Hester, who had married Major Leonard M. E. Dent D.S.O. in July 1920.[314] These were Celia (born 1922), Rosalind (1923), Anita (1925), Gerard (1928) and Theresa (1930). Henry was seldom happier than when he had youngsters around him.

As part of his grieving over George's death, Henry wanted to find out as much as he could about George's war time service and particularly the events in March 1918. With Francis, he took a journey across to Belgium and France in July 1921, visiting the bleak battlefields of Ypres and the Somme. The journey was made pleasanter by some time spent with Albertine and Louis Quarles van Ufford in Breukelen, including celebrating Henry's 70th birthday. The photograph of Henry opposite was taken in Breukelen on this visit.[315]

On his return home, Henry was unable to carry out his normal duties due to further ill health. Following medical advice, he decided that he should resign from editing the Parish Magazine, writing:

> Mr. Willink is very sorry to announce that he cannot continue to run the magazine after next December. The Editorship which he undertook jointly with Mrs. Willink in October 1917 has been a pleasure and an interest to him during these four years, and he has done his best to make this little paper worthy of the parish. But this has meant a good deal of trouble, besides being a tie and an expense. And being seriously advised to curtail his activities he feels that this is one of the things which he must give up. He thanks many friends for kind support, and trusts that someone will be found to "carry on" – for Burghfield ought not to be without a Magazine.[316]

This did not mean that Henry was withdrawing from local involvement in the parish now that he had entered his 70s. He had been elected to the first Parochial Church Council (PCC) of St. Mary's, following the reorganisation of the governance of the Anglican Church in 1920, being appointed PCC Hon. Secretary and Treasurer a year later. In addition, he continued as churchwarden (which position he resigned in 1924)[317] and was chairman of the Trustees of the Old School, of the Burghfield United Charities, and of the School Managers, and a Trustee of Mrs. Bland's School.[318]

Henry continued to work hard to support and improve education in the county through his work chairing the Berkshire Education Committee. In 1923 Henry was instrumental in bringing forward the first Free Public Libraries in Berkshire. The scheme, adopted by the Berkshire County Council in July 1923, was to establish a central book store, employ a librarian, and gradually create a number of local centres for the public to borrow the books. These centres, initially at least, were the elementary schools where the head teachers had agreed to facilitate the process.[319]

Before long, Burghfield had its own library centre in the New Schools. Henry no doubt used many opportunities to encourage use of the library, as on the occasion below:

> On the eve of breaking up for the holidays the certificates for the year ending 31st March were presented. There were present Mr. H. G. Willink and Mr. Lousley, with the Rector and Mrs. Johnson.
>
> Mr. Willink spoke to the children, urging them to remember that education is not finished on leaving school, and that, with the County Library available, everyone in the Parish has the opportunity of reading to increase their knowledge.[320]

Henry was still able to enjoy hills – although alpine mountains were now a thing of the past! In early 1928, he wrote of a recent visit to his much beloved Lake District:

> The last occasion was at Easter 1926, when (aged 75) I walked with a family party from and to Buttermere, *via* Scale Force, right along the ridge of Red Pike, High Stile, and High Crag in lovely weather. These "gigantic peaks" were undoubtedly loftier and more precipitous than they used to be, as well as further apart, but they still yielded to treatment, slowly and steadily applied. Yet the joy of hurling oneself down steep slopes of rough ground is gone. Such raptures have faded away and are ill replaced by the stiffly cautious movements of advancing age.
>
> Nevertheless, hardly a visit fails to leave some "sweete memories." The resources of Lakeland seem to be inexhaustible. As the ability to climb and roam at will diminishes, the loss seems to be compensated by delights and interests of a less strenuous kind. If a 12-hour grind of crags has become too stiff for stiffening septuagenarian muscles, these same muscles may still (by the help of a naughty motor) be up to an afternoon walk along the hippopotamus backs of the rounded ranges between Sedbergh and Low Borrow Bridge, getting back to dinner at Burneside.[321]

The destination mentioned at the end of the passage above – Burneside – was the home of Henry's first cousin Alfred Willink, with whom he often went walking. In the late 1890s, Henry had designed a weathervane for Alfred's house:

Burneside Weather-Stork
n: Kendal
designed by HGW.

It is highly probable that Henry also designed the weathervane for Hillfields that incorporated parts of the Willink shield. In the course of time, this weathervane had become the property of Mr. Gerard Dent, Henry's great-nephew. Mr. Dent then kindly donated the vane to The Willink School where, following its restoration by Mr. Colin Burnett, it now tops the "New Block," visible from Hollybush Lane in Burghfield Common.

Hillfields
Weathervane
at
The Willink
School

Family gatherings at Hillfields, generally in the long school holidays, were delightful times for the younger generation. By this date the house was lit, not by gas, but by DC electricity generated by a diesel engine, started at 6 o'clock every morning by Pembroke, the chauffeur – known to all as "Pem." The house, filled with many curiosities, was like a fascinating museum to the young visitors.

Life at Hillfields was accompanied by the sound of Alpine bells. Each of Henry's Jersey cows had a bell that he had brought specially from his travels in Switzerland, with each one sounding its own individual note. The cows were all named, of course, although only two names are still remembered: Daisy and Queenie.

With its own cattle, Hillfields produced its own milk, cream and butter. Leela, the cook, happily let the children into the buttery to watch the butter being made.

Family gatherings in the Lake District continued to be an important feature of Henry's life. His grandson Charles recalls being taken by Ba up his first real hill, Green Gable, near Great Gable, when he was just 7 years old. Henry cheerfully nicknamed Charles "Great Gabble," saying he never stopped talking.

A very touching tribute appeared in the June 1926 Parish Magazine, written by Henry, in memory of Miss Georgina Brown, known to the family as "Na," who had died on 12 May. Henry wrote:

Miss Brown entered Mr. and Mrs. Willink's household in London about 1882, and came with them as children's nurse to Highwoods in 1890 and on to Hillfields in 1893. She helped to nurse Mrs. Willink through her last illness, and stayed on with Mr. Willink until about a year ago, when she retired into private life in London, coming down to Burghfield from time to time, especially when the "children" or grandchildren were here, to whom she was devoted. For years, she had been one of the most useful members of the Women's Institute, and in every possible way has taken her full share of parochial activities. She was a good Churchwoman and a Burghfield parishioner at heart. By the kindness of the Rector her wish to be buried in Burghfield churchyard was fulfilled, where she lies close to her beloved mistress and friend.[322]

Rector and Churchwardens
of St. Mary's Church, Burghfield
Photograph taken in 1922

Left to right:
Mr. Job Lousley, Rev. W. H. George, HGW

Henry was Churchwarden from 1910 to 1924

The next major event for Henry was the marriage of his son Francis on Wednesday 7 May 1930. Francis was 39 years old, and his bride, Alma Marion Chignell (known as Marion), just 20. The marriage took place in St. Wilfred's Church, Northenden, Cheshire, where Marion's father was Rector.

It was a beautiful and happy wedding, with crowds of relatives and friends on both sides. And the weather was kind and nearly as bright as on the occasion of the marriage of the bridegroom's sister (so well remembered in Burghfield), Mrs. Catharine D. Pilkington with Major Edward F. Pilkington on 28th January 1914. Mr. Denis Pilkington (Major Pilkington's brother) acted

147

as best man. The bride's train-bearers were Master Michael Pilkington and the Misses Celia and Rosalind Dent, respectively nephew and cousins of the bridegroom; while among the six bridesmaids were his two nieces, the Misses Noel and Honor Pilkington and Miss Margaret Chignell, sister of the bride.

The happy pair have been spending the honeymoon in Venice and the Alps, returning via Holland in order to pay a short visit to Dutch relations of Mr. Willink… He [Francis] is now a Managing Director in the Manchester Collieries Ltd., and has fortunately secured a house ("Highfield," Worsley) about as near to Manchester one side as Northenden is on the other, so that his wife will not be separated far from her parents, nor he from his sister. We are sure that all in Burghfield wish them health and happiness.[323]

In early 1932, Henry became Vice President of the Council of Reading University, a position he retained until 1937.[324] He had first become involved with the governance of University College, as it was then known, in 1905 and so in all his association spanned 32 years.

A few weeks later, in April 1932, Henry resigned from the Chairmanship of the Berkshire Education Committee. The committee resolved:

That we, the Education Committee of the Berkshire County Council, hereby express our sincere regret for the retirement of Mr. H. G. Willink from the office of Chairman, a post which he has held for the past 24 years from 1908 until now, and place upon record our grateful thanks for his long, faithful, and efficient service.[325]

The Parish Magazine added to the tribute that "we do not think anyone in the county has done more good work for the schools than Mr. Willink, if we may be permitted to say so." In the same edition of the magazine, it stated that Henry was re-elected as Vice Chairman of the Parochial Church Council of St. Mary's, a post he held from 1931 to 1935.[326]

HGW's sketch of Francis and Marion's house, Highfield
The original is a watercolour

September 1932

Resigning the Chairmanship of the Education Committee did not relieve him of attendance at any Sub-committees though, as he remained a member of all nine of them, and continued to chair the School Management Sub-committee.

Henry suffered another prolonged bout of illness through the autumn of 1932, which seems to have lasted well into 1933 as he was still absent from meetings up to February.[327] He visited Katie and Ned and his four grandchildren in April in their new home of Dunham Oaks, Bowdon, Cheshire.

HGW's watercolour of Dunham Oaks
September 1936

In June, Henry was well enough to travel to the Lake District and sketch some wild scenery. On this trip, he climbed Coniston Old Man – and considered it fitting that that should be his last Lake District climb! [328]

Even in 1936, aged 85, Henry could walk down Snowdon, though he had needed the train to get up to the top. This was his last time in the hills and mountains.

Henry wrote a 103-page biography of his father, William Williamson Willink, in 1936 and had copies printed privately, distributing them among the family and to some friends. This is a well-written and very interesting account, showing that

Henry had certainly not lost his ability to master his subject and order his material, or to write fluently and well. This volume, together with both the *Dictionary of National Biography* entry (1894 edition) and the biography he wrote of his grandfather Sir George Nicholls (in *History of the English Poor Law* 1897), show his love for his family as well as his literary skill.

During these last years, Henry gradually reduced his workload by withdrawing from various committees and Boards. Just a couple more deserve some mention.

In November 1936, Henry resigned the office of Honorary Treasurer of the Burghfield Lodge of Oddfellows. He had been their treasurer for so long that no-one – including Henry himself – was quite sure how long it had been. The social gathering to celebrate the Lodge's 70th anniversary thanked him profusely for "about 45 years' service." [329]

In early 1938, with growing infirmity, Henry relinquished the work that was perhaps closest to his heart – membership of the Education Committee.[330] After his death, Mr. A. P. Shaw (Chairman of the Education Committee in succession to Henry) paid tribute to Henry's work by saying:

> All of us feel that the foundation which he laid in our local education was one that will remain and will be a sound one on which to build in the future. He was a man whom all respected, and whom we all, I might say, loved. He was just and kind to everyone with whom he came into contact. Everyone who met him felt that they obtained help and inspiration from his acquaintance. His public services were many.

Mr. J. W. Walker, who worked with Henry on the Higher Education Sub-committee, wrote that Henry's:

> abilities, education, artistic powers and high moral principles made up a personality the like of which are none too numerous in our public life. His services to the education of the county

have been of outstanding and permanent value. He had a large share in laying down the lines on which Berkshire education has proceeded and not only in its initial stages, but right on to the end he identified himself with the work of our schools. He was a valued governor of several of them, and was ever the friend of the teacher and encourager of the pupil. He was an artist of no mean ability, and here again he delighted to encourage the budding artists of our schools, by offering prizes, and assisting in judging in connection with scholars' art work. If educational work in Berkshire is, as I think it is, something of which the county may be proud, it behoves us to remember those who did so much in the past to start it on right lines, and of those the name of Mr. Willink will ever stand amongst the foremost.[331]

Henry resigned from the Athenaeum Club in London in 1937, and the Club took the highly unusual step of electing him a life member. He retained his membership of the Berkshire Club in Reading to the end of his life.[332]

And so we come to Henry's final moments. He died peacefully at Hillfields in the early hours of Saturday 30 April 1938 surrounded by family. The causes of death were heart failure, failure to drain bronchial secretions, and kidney failure.[333] He was 86 years old.

Henry's funeral was on the following Tuesday, 3 May, at St. Mary's Church, Burghfield. The service was taken by Rev. J. D. Ouvry, his brother-in-law, Rev. H. Chignell, Francis's father-in-law, and Rev. Harvey W. G. Thursby. The reading was the same as that read by Henry at the Dedication of the Memorial Cross in 1920, with a few extra verses included:

Wisdom 3: 1-9

But the souls of the righteous are in the hand of God, and no torment will ever touch them. In the eyes of the foolish they seemed to have died, and their departure was thought to be an affliction, and their going from us to be their destruction; but they are at peace. For though in the sight of men they were punished, their hope is full of immortality. Having been disciplined a little, they will receive great good, because God tested them and found them worthy of himself; like gold in the furnace he tried them, and like a sacrificial burnt offering he accepted them. In the time of their visitation they will shine forth, and will run like sparks through the stubble. They will govern nations and rule over peoples, and the Lord will reign over them for ever. Those who trust in him will understand truth, and the faithful will abide with him in love, because grace and mercy are upon his elect, and he watches over his holy ones. [334]

Many of the Willink, Ouvry, Pilkington, Clark and Dent family were present, including several who had come across from the Netherlands. Henry would have approved that, in the list of family mourners, members of his household staff were named. The list of those attending the ceremony, from the Lord Lieutenant of Berkshire (Mr. A. T. Lloyd) downwards, was very long and distinguished.

Two of Henry's favourite hymns were sung: "O God, our help in ages past," and "When all Thy mercies, O my God, my rising soul surveys," the latter being less well known now. Psalms 23 ("The Lord is my shepherd") and 121 ("I will lift up mine eyes unto the hills") were chanted, with the second psalm being very appropriate for Henry's love of such scenery. The service concluded with the *Nunc Dimittis*, "Lord, now lettest Thou Thy servant depart in peace." [335]

Henry was buried in St. Mary's churchyard with his beloved Mary. When Henry had arranged for Mary's gravestone to be erected, as is usual in such circumstances, space had been left on the memorial cross for Henry's name. It was added in due course.

Henry's estate amounted to £90,165 15s 11d. He gave his daughter Katie £2,000. He left just £20 to his "dear son-in-law, Edward Fielden Pilkington, he having already received on January 28, 1914, the best gift which it was in my power to bestow."

153

He made numerous bequests to the younger generation –
for example £100 to Hester Dent and £50 to each of her
children. He "forgave all loans made to relatives and friends."

Mary Grace Willink
1850 – 1918
Henry George Willink
1851 – 1938

To his driver, his "good friend and faithful servant" George Pembroke, Henry gave £500 and half a month's wages for each year of service. To other servants he gave a month's wages. Henry gave a year's rent to each rent-paying tenant at Burghfield.

He donated £300 to the University of Reading and £50 to the Eton Fund.

The residue of the estate, including Hillfields, went to his son, Francis.[336]

Memorial tablet to Henry
on the north wall of St. Mary's Church, Burghfield

Hillfields
by John Piper
(1903 – 1992)

Major Leonard M. E. Dent D.S.O. &
Hester Dent, née Clark, HGW's niece

Epilogue

Hillfields

A Professor on a T-table

he "only visitor to Hillfields who has honestly claimed to like its architecture is Mr. John Betjeman," at least in the opinion of the *Antique Collector* in its August 1964 edition. Perhaps the artist John Piper should be added, as he took the pains to paint it.[337]

The ownership of Hillfields, as we have seen, passed from Henry to his son Francis. However, Francis lived and worked near Manchester, and, much as he loved his childhood home, he was settled with his wife in Highfield in Worsley. The solution was to sell the house to a willing member of the family. Hillfields was bought from Francis by Major Leonard Dent, husband of Henry's niece Hester, in 1939.[338]

Leonard and Hester Dent and their children had stayed at Hillfields many times and all loved it dearly. Major Dent subsequently filled the house with a remarkable collection of antique furniture, silver, paintings and watercolours, including a notable collection of drawings and watercolours by Thomas Rowlandson.

Hillfields passed from family ownership, a hundred years after Henry bought it, when it was purchased and extensively renovated by The Guide Dogs for the Blind Association, who moved their headquarters into the house in 1992.[339]

157

A Biography of H. G. Willink 1851 – 1938

Acknowledgements

An I Glass

would not have been in contact with members of the Willink family if it had not been for Major John Steeds, who therefore merits my first thanks! I would also like to thank Mary Hancock for conversations about local history.

Gerard Dent, son of Hester and Leonard Dent, has enthusiastically supported this work throughout. I enjoyed meeting his older sister, Celia, who shared her memories of Ba from her youth. It was a privilege to talk with Henry's grandson, Rev. Charles G. W. Pilkington, who is well into his 90s, who shared his memories of visits to Hillfields and of family holidays with his grandfather in his beloved Lake District. I felt within touching distance of the living Henry George Willink, since all three had known him personally.

I owe a very large debt of thanks to Henry's great granddaughter Janet and her husband Duncan, for hospitality when my wife and I visited them and for their generosity in lending me several treasures. This book would have been much the poorer in many ways without Janet's mother Noel's copy of Henry's biography of his father, and the many images from Henry's sketchbooks that either were in their possession or had been borrowed from the family, and not least three of Henry's photograph albums. My thanks also go to them for reading the draft text of the book and helping to improve it.

Lastly, I'd like to thank my wife, Cathy, for all her support throughout this project and for her patient proofreading skills. I have dedicated the book to her because I think she embodies the Willink motto – *Fides et Amor*.

A Biography of H. G. Willink 1851 – 1938

Endnotes & Sources

[1] The minutes of this meeting can be found at the Berkshire Record Office document reference C/EM 92 "Burghfield Willink School Governors' Meetings April 1956 to May 1965."

[2] Statement by Mr. Noel Jackson, first Headmaster of The Willink School.

[3] This portrait is taken from the frontispiece of *Memoir of William Williamson Willink* by H. G. Willink (Privately printed 1836). In the text the date for the portrait is given as three or four years after the subject's death. It was produced using a previous unsuccessful portrait of about 1873 and some photographs. William is therefore shown at about 65 years of age, ten years before his death.

[4] Henry's birth was announced in several newspapers, for example *Liverpool Mercury* 22 July 1851 p5 column 1 and *London Evening Standard* 19 July 1851 p4 column 6. The latter states: "BIRTHS. On the 10th inst., at Liverpool, the wife of W. W. Willink, Esq., of a son."

[5] Catharine's Death Certificate states: "Fifteenth July 1851 at Princes Park, in the Sub-District of Toxteth Park, Catharine Harriet Willink aged 26, wife of William Williamson Willink Vice Consul of the Netherlands, of Scarlet Fever. Registered Seventeenth July 1851, informant Elizabeth Windle, present at the Death." (Elizabeth Windle was one of three servants at the Willink's house in Princes Park, according to the 1851 census.)

Catharine's burial details can be found in Huyton Parish Bishop's Transcripts Burials 1851 "Catherine (sic) Harriet Willink of Toxteth Park, buried 22 July aged 26 years." Collection "Lancashire, England, Church of England Deaths and Burials, 1813-1986" https://www.ancestry.co.uk accessed January 2017. Also, see *Memoir of William Williamson Willink* by H. G. Willink (Privately printed 1936) p43-44.

[6] Henry's baptism record can be found in St. John the Baptist, Princes Park Parish Record 1851 July 23 "Henry George son of William Williamson (Vice Consul of the Netherlands) & Catharine Harriet Willink of Princes Park." William's brother, Rev. Arthur Willink, officiated. Collection "Liverpool, England, Church of England Baptisms, 1813-1906" https://www.ancestry.co.uk accessed January 2017.

[7] 1841 Census (6 June) Class HO 107, Piece 567, Book 10, Civil Parish Toxteth Park in the County of Lancashire, Enumeration District 42, Folio 39 Page 20 Line 5. This record actually does not have Daniel in – perhaps he was abroad at the time. Note that the ages were rounded in the 1841 census. The household contained:

Ann Willink, aged 50, Living on Independent Means
William Willink, aged 30, Engineer
Clara Willink, aged 20

Catherine Willink, aged 20

Jacob Willink, aged 20, Merchant

Arthur Willink, aged 15.

[8] *Memoir of William Williamson Willink* by H. G. Willink (Privately printed 1936) p6

[9] Ibid. and endpaper.

[10] Daniel Willink was born on 29 July 1779, the second son of Wilhem and Hester Willink. The date is given in *History of the Family of Willink of Willink-Hof* by William Williamson Willink (1847 with later additions) p12 and https://www.genealogieonline.nl accessed January 2017. Wilhem was a leading figure in Amsterdam, mainly due to his successful Mercantile House (which for many years was the Banker in Europe of the United States of America, a role subsequently taken over by Barings).

[11] The certificate is given in the London Metropolitan Archives, St. Giles, Camberwell, Register of Marriages P73/GIS Item 014, available in the collection "London, England, Marriages and Banns, 1754-1921" https://www.ancestry.co.uk accessed January 2017. The certificate states "Daniel Willink Esq of the Parish of St. James, Westminster, bachelor, & Anne Latham of this parish, spinster, a minor, were married in this church by licence this sixteenth day of March 1808." Also in *Salisbury and Winchester Journal* 21 March 1808 p3 column 3: MARRIED: "- Same day [Wednesday 16 March], Daniel Willink, Esq., of Amsterdam, to Miss Ann (sic) Latham, daughter of Thomas Latham, Esq., of Champion-hill, Camberwell."

[12] William Williamson Willink: born 9 December 1808 (date of birth given on his baptism record 25 December 1808 St. Giles, Camberwell), collection "London Metropolitan Archives, St Giles, Camberwell, Composite register: baptisms Jul 1802 - Dec 1812, burials 1800 - Dec 1812, P73/GIS/002" https://www.ancestry.co.uk accessed January 2017.   The story of his baptismal names can be found in *Memoir of William Williamson Willink* by H. G. Willink (Privately printed 1936) p8 and 9.

[13] *Memoir of William Williamson Willink* by H. G. Willink (Privately printed 1836) p9.

[14] The announcement was made in the *Lancaster Gazette* 26 March 1814 p3 column 4. The date of his appointment (20 January 1814) is given in *History of the Family of Willink of Willink-Hof* by William Williamson Willink (1847 with later additions) p13.

[15] *History of the Family of Willink of Willink-Hof* by William Williamson Willink (1847 with later additions) p17.

[16] Daniel and Anne's children were:

1st William Williamson Willink: born 9 December 1808 (date of birth given on his baptism record 25 December 1808 St. Giles, Camberwell);

died aged 75 on 11 December 1883 (date of death given in his entry in the England & Wales National Probate Calendar for 1884);

2nd Anne Willink: born 31 December 1809 (date of birth given on her baptism record 22 January 1810 St. Mary, Marylebone, London); died aged 16 on 1 Apr 1826 in Liverpool (*Gore's Liverpool General Advertiser* 6 April 1826 p3 column 6);

3rd John Abraham Willink: born 6 August 1811 (date of birth given on his baptism record 29 August 1811 St. Mary Magdalen, Richmond, Surrey); died January 1812 aged 5 months in Richmond (burial record 27 January 1812 St. Mary Magdalen, Richmond, Surrey);

4th Hester Alice Willink: born on 22 July 1813 in Liverpool (date of birth given on her baptism record 17 August 1813 Holy Trinity, Liverpool); died aged 24, five months after her marriage to William Robertson Sandbach in Paris in October 1837 (burial record in UK, Foreign and Overseas Registers of British Subjects 1628-1969 29 October 1837);

5th Clara Cecilia Willink: born about March 1816 (baptism record 15 March 1816 Toxteth Park, Liverpool); died aged 31 on 6 July 1847 in Barn Hey, Toxteth Park, Liverpool (*Liverpool Mercury* 9 July 1847 p7 column 4);

6th Catharina Mary Willink: born about May 1818 (baptism record 28 May 1818 St. Philip, Liverpool); married John Orred 6 June 1843 St. Mary, Edge Hill, Liverpool (*Liverpool Mercury* 9 June 1843 p2 column 5); died aged 40 at the end of June 1858 (burial record 2 July 1858 St. Mary's, Marshfield, Gloucestershire);

7th Jacob Willink: born on 13 July 1819 in Liverpool (date of birth at https://www.genealogieonline.nl accessed January 2017) baptised at St. Philip's, Liverpool, on 21 September 1819; died 15 August 1901 aged 82 in Chappel, Essex (Probate Record in Index of Wills and Administrations 1858-1966 for 1901);

8th Arthur Willink: born 27 March 1824 in Liverpool (date of birth given on his baptism record 28 April 1824 St. Philip, Liverpool); died 21 November 1862 aged 38 in Madeira, Portugal (Probate Record in Index of Wills and Administrations 1858-1966 for 1863);

9th & 10th One stillborn boy and one girl who survived just 4 hours after birth, *History of the Family of Willink of Willink-Hof* by William Williamson Willink (1847 with later additions) p12.

[17] See *History of the Family of Willink of Willink-Hof* by William Williamson Willink (1847 with later additions) p15. In *Gore's Liverpool Directory* 1827 p338 it gives the address: "Willink Daniel, Esq., merchant and Consul for the Netherlands, 61 Rodney Street; offices 3 Goree Piazzas. The house is described in an advertisement in *Gore's Liverpool General Advertiser* 12 November 1829 p1 column 1.

[18] *History of the Family of Willink of Willink-Hof* by William Williamson Willink (1847 with later additions) p13.

[19] For a description of the house, see the advertisement in *Gore's Liverpool General Advertiser* 5 March 1840 p1 column 2.

[20] *Memoir of William Williamson Willink* by H. G. Willink (Privately printed 1836) p22.

[21] Ibid. p11.

[22] Advertisements in *Gore's Liverpool General Advertiser* 7 August 1828 p2 column 1, 13 January 1831 p2 column 6, and 6 July 1837 p1 column 6.

[23] *Memoir of William Williamson Willink* by H. G. Willink (Privately printed 1836) p16 – 17. The jewel is still in the possession of the family.

[24] Ibid. p26, 28 – 29.

[25] Ibid. p29 – 30.

[26] *History of the Family of Willink of Willink-Hof* by William Williamson Willink, (1847 with later additions) p14.

[27] The honour is given in *Burke's Peerage, Baronetage and Knightage*, 107th edition, volume 3 p4189 www.thepeerage.com, accessed January 2017; the date is given in *History of the Family of Willink of Willink-Hof* by William Williamson Willink, (1847 with later additions) p14; Daniel styled himself with the title, for example in *Gore's Liverpool General Advertiser* 28 May 1846 p1 column 4: "NOTICE.- The undersigned, Knight of the Order of the Netherland Lion, Consul of his Majesty the King of the Netherlands, Prince of Orange Nassau, Grand Duke of Luxembourg, &c. &c. &c...."

[28] *Memoir of William Williamson Willink* by H. G. Willink (Privately printed 1836) p33, 35.

[29] Information about George Nicholls in this section, unless otherwise noted, is taken from *Life of Sir George Nicholls* by Henry George Willink, published in the first volume of *History of the English Poor Law* by Sir George Nicholls, revised by H. G. Willink (London 1898). An obituary of Sir George Nicholls can be found in the *Illustrated London News* 1 April 1865 p21 column 3. The entry in the *Dictionary of National Biography*, Volume 14 pages 438-441, was also written by Henry.

[30] Harriet Maltby was born on 10 April 1786. See the collection "England, Select Births and Christenings, 1538-1975" https://www.ancestry.co.uk accessed January 2017.

[31] George Nicholls married Harriet Maltby on 6 July 1813. Details can be found in *Visitation of England and Wales* Volume 2 Edited by Joseph Jackson Howard and Frederick Arthur Crisp (1894) p49. This can be viewed at https://archive.org accessed January 2017.

[32] George and Harriet Nicholls children were:

    1st Georgiana Elizabeth Nicholls: born 23 June 1814 at Southwell, Notts;

died aged 86 on 4 May 1901 at 3 Hyde Park Street, Paddington, London. She was the first child to be born and the last to die. She remained unmarried;

2nd Charlotte Nicholls: born 16 May 1816 at Farndon, Nottinghamshire; married Rev. William Frederick Wingfield 2 November 1844 at St. John's Church, Paddington; died 17 November 1880, aged 64, at Slindon in Sussex;

3rd Emily Nicholls: born 28 October 1817 at Farndon, Nottinghamshire; died aged 17 on 19 March 1835 in London;

4th Jane Nicholls: born 20 May 1819 in Southwell, Nottinghamshire; married Rev. Peter Thomas Ouvry 21 July 1846 at St. John's Church, Paddington; died aged 36 on 8 January 1856 at Wing, Buckinghamshire. Jane was Henry's wife's mother;

5th Mary Grace Nicholls: born 17 July 1820 in Southwell, Nottinghamshire; died aged 14, nine days after her sister Emily on 28 March 1835;

6th Henry George Nicholls: born 10 January 1822 in Southwell; he became an ordained minister; he married his first cousin Caroline Maria Nicholls on 17 August 1853 in Tiverton, Devon; he died aged 44 on 1 January 1867 at 24 Porchester Terrace, London;

7th Harriet Nicholls: born 21 January 1823 and died 17 March the same year, at Southwell, Nottinghamshire;

8th Catharine Harriet Nicholls: born 29 August 1824 at Longford House, Gloucester; married William Williamson Willink on 4 June 1844 at St. John's Church, Paddington; died 15 July 1851 at Princes Park, Toxteth Park near Liverpool. Catherine was Henry's mother.

The details in this note can all be found in *Visitation of England and Wales* Volume 2 Edited by Joseph Jackson Howard and Frederick Arthur Crisp (1894) p49-51. This can be viewed at https://archive.org accessed January 2017.

[33] George Nicholls: C.B. awarded 27 April 1848 – see the *London Gazette* 28 April 1848 Issue 20850 p1655 column 2. For his K.C.B. – see the *London Gazette* 4 March 1851 Issue 21188 p634 col 1. The presentation of the honour was reported in the *Hampshire Chronicle* 9 August 1851 p8 column 3.

[34] William and Catharine's marriage certificate can be viewed in the collection "London Metropolitan Archives, Saint John the Evangelist, Paddington, register of marriages, P87/JNE1, Item 008" https://www.ancestry.co.uk accessed January 2017. The marriage is noted also in the *Liverpool Mail* 8 June 1844 p7 column 6: "On the 4th instant, at St. John's Church, Paddington, by the Rev. Wm. Wingfield, W. W. Willink, Esq., of Liverpool, to Catherine (sic) Harriet, youngest daughter of George

Nicholls, Esq., of Hyde Park-street." Rev. William Frederick Wingfield married Charlotte Nicholls, Catharine Harriet Nicholls's sister, five months later in November 1844. Thus, he became brother-in-law to William and Charlotte.

To add to the family links, the curate of St John's, Paddington, at the time was Rev. Peter Thomas Ouvry, who married another sister, Jane Nicholls, in July 1846.

[35] *Memoir of William Williamson Willink* by H. G. Willink (Privately printed 1936) p40.

[36] Harriet Anne's baptism can be found at Liverpool Record Office, document 283 HAM/2/2. It can be viewed in the collection "Liverpool, England, Baptisms 1813-1906" https://www.ancestry.co.uk accessed January 2017. This shows St. Michael in the Hamlet Parish Record for 1845 October 16 (at a private baptism) "Harriet Anne daughter of William Williamson (Merchant) & Catherine (sic) Harriet Willink of Roby Parish, Huyton." A marginal note states "born at St. Michael's, Toxteth, 11 October 1845."

Harriet Anne's burial details can be viewed in the collection "Lancashire, England, Deaths and Burials, 1813-1986" https://www.ancestry.co.uk accessed January 2017. This gives the Bishop's Transcript for Huyton 1846 "Harriet Anne Willink of Roby, buried on August 26th, aged 10 months. Officiating minister P. T. Ouvry." Rev. Peter Thomas Ouvry was Catharine Willink's brother-in-law, having married her sister Jane in July 1846 – see Note 33 above.

[37] *Memoir of William Williamson Willink* by H. G. Willink (Privately printed 1936) p41 – 42.

[38] Ibid. p32.

[39] Ibid. p8.

[40] Ibid. p50 – 51.

[41] Ibid. p51.

[42] Advertised in the *Liverpool Mail* 9 June 1855 p1 column 6.

[43] *Memoir of William Williamson Willink* by H. G. Willink (Privately printed 1936) p52.

[44] Advertisement in the *Morning Post* 19 June 1844 p8 column 5.

[45] *A Passion for Nature: 19th century Naturalism in the Circle of Charles Alexander Johns* by Deirdre Dare and Melissa Hardie, Patten Press 2008 p141.

[46] *Memoir of William Williamson Willink* by H. G. Willink (Privately printed 1936) p52.

[47] Ibid. p53.

[48] Ibid. p56.

[49] Ibid. p52. Also, see the notice in the *Hampshire Chronicle* 11 July 1863 p4 column 3.

166

[50] *Memoir of William Williamson Willink* by H. G. Willink (Privately printed 1936) p58 – 59.

[51] *The Eton Register Part III 1862-1868*, Eton 1906, published by Spottiswoode & Co, p57 and 77, available online at https://archive.org accessed January 2017. The abbreviation F.V. by Henry's name in the Register means F. Vidal's House. Similarly, the W.J. means that his Tutor was William Johnson (later known as William Cory).

[52] *A Memoir of Henry Bradshaw* by G. W. Prothero, London 1888, published by Kegan Paul, Trench & Co, p130.

[53] *Reminiscences* by Arthur Duke Coleridge, London 1921, published by Constable & Co, p58.

[54] *Pall Mall Gazette* 25 November 1868 p7 column 1.

[55] *The Eton Boating Book* 3rd Edition, Eton 1933, published by Spottiswoode, Ballantyne & Co., p154; *Evening Mail (London)* 5 June 1867 p8 column 4.

[56] *The Eton Boating Book* 3rd Edition, Eton 1933, published by Spottiswoode, Ballantyne & Co., p161; also in the *London Evening Standard* 5 June 1868 p6 column 2.

[57] *The Eton Boating Book* 3rd Edition, Eton 1933, published by Spottiswoode, Ballantyne & Co., p164.

[58] *Memoir of William Williamson Willink* by H. G. Willink (Privately printed 1936) p83.

[59] *The Eton Boating Book* 3rd Edition, Eton 1933, published by Spottiswoode, Ballantyne & Co., p168; also in the *London Evening Standard* 5 June 1869 p3 column 3.

[60] *Memoir of William Williamson Willink* by H. G. Willink (Privately printed 1936) p83.

[61] *In Memoriam* in the *Alpine Journal*, Volume 50 p283.

[62] Ibid.

[63] *Memoir of William Williamson Willink* by H. G. Willink (Privately printed 1936) p83 and *Berkshire Chronicle* 24 December 1869 p8 column 3.

[64] Henry's College and subjects of study are given in the obituary *In Memoriam* in the *Alpine Journal*, Volume 50 p284; an entry on Henry can also be found in *Alumni Oxonienses: The Members of the University of Oxford 1715-1886* Volume IV by Joseph Foster, published by James Parker & Co., Oxford 1891 p1576. This book can be found online at https://archive.org accessed January 2017.

[65] *In Memoriam* in the *Alpine Journal*, Volume 50 p284.

[66] Ibid. p283; *Memoir of William Williamson Willink* by H. G. Willink (Privately printed 1936) p64 – 65.

[67] *Memoir of William Williamson Willink* by H. G. Willink (Privately printed 1936) p68.

[68] Ibid. p81.
[69] Ibid. p76.
[70] *In Memoriam* in the *Alpine Journal*, Volume 50 p283.
[71] *Memoir of William Williamson Willink* by H. G. Willink (Privately printed 1936) p78.
[72] Ibid. p80.
[73] *In Memoriam* in the *Alpine Journal*, Volume 50 p283; *Memoir of William Williamson Willink* by H. G. Willink (Privately printed 1936) p77 – 78.
[74] *Memoir of William Williamson Willink* by H. G. Willink (Privately printed 1936) p84 – 85.
[75] Ibid. p81 – 82, 85.
[76] *The Fell and Rock Climbing Club of the English Lake District* Vol. 8 No. 1, 1928, p12-13.
[77] Ibid. p13-14.
[78] Ibid. p14.
[79] The result is reported in the *Morning Post* 20 June 1872 p3 column 5; also in *Men-at-the Bar* by Joseph Foster, Second Edition, 1885 London, published by Hazell, Watson and Viney, p511. This is available online at https://archive.org accessed January 2017.
[80] Daniel Willink died aged 79 at Barn Hey, Aigburth Road, Liverpool on 6 January 1859. This was reported in the *Evening Mail (London)* 10 January 1859 p8 column 6 and *Morning Chronicle* 11 January 1859 p8 column 5.

Sir George Nicholls died aged 83 on 24 March 1865 at 17 Hyde Park Street, Paddington – *London Evening Standard* 27 March 1865 p7 column 6.

Harriet Nicholls (née Maltby) died aged 83 on 14 May 1869 at 17 Hyde Park Street, Paddington – *Pall Mall Gazette* 15 May 1869 p6 column 2.

Anne Willink (née Latham) died aged 81 on 8 November 1870 at Barn Hey, Aigburth Road, Liverpool – *Liverpool Mail* 12 November 1870 p12 column 4.
[81] 1861 Census (7 April) Class: RG 9; Piece 8; Folio: 36; Page 20, Parish: St. John's, Paddington. On this date, 16 Hyde Park Street contained:
William W. Willink, Head of Household, aged 52, widower, Civil Service – Secretary Public Works Loan Commission
Henry G. Willink, son, aged 9, Scholar
Anne Willink, mother, aged 71, Lady
Mary Corbett, Lady's servant, aged 30
George Wiggans, Butler, aged 34
Eleanor Roberts, Cook, aged 48
Martha Adams, Housemaid, aged 35
17 Hyde Park Street contained:
George Nicholls, Head of Household, aged 79, Knight of the Bath
Harriet Nicholls, wife, aged 74

Georgiana Nicholls, daughter, aged 46
George Hillier, Butler, aged 45
Hannah Chandler, Cook, aged 38
Ellen Warren, Housemaid, aged 28
Hannah Jarvis, Lady's Maid, aged 36
Julia Church, Housemaid, aged 26
Henry's brother, William Nicholls Willink (aged 13), was at school –
Stubbington House, Titchfield, Hampshire, on this date.
[82] 1871 Census (2 April): Class: RG10; Piece: 21; Folio: 18; Page: 27;
Parish: St. John's, Paddington. On this date, 3 Hyde Park Street contained:
  William W. Willink, Head of Household, aged 62, widower, Secretary
  Public Works
  William Willink, son, aged 23, Gentleman
  Henry G. Willink, son, aged 19, Undergraduate
  Georgiana Nicholls, sister-in-law, aged 50, Gentlewoman
  George Wiggans, Butler, aged 44
  Mary Ann Hyde, Cook, aged 34
  Malinda Bobby, Lady's Maid, aged 28
  Martha Adams, Housemaid, aged 45
  Elizabeth Pilbeam, Kitchenmaid, aged 16.
[83] *Memoir of William Williamson Willink* by H. G. Willink (Privately
printed 1936) p87.
[84] *Men-at-the Bar* by Joseph Foster, Second Edition, 1885 London,
published by Hazell, Watson and Viney, p511. This is available online at
https://archive.org accessed January 2017.
[85] Online at http://www.lincolnsinn.org.uk accessed January 2017.
[86] *In Memoriam* in the *Alpine Journal*, Volume 50 p285; it is also claimed
in two further obituaries: *The Times* 5 May 1938 Issue 47986 p18 column
C and in the *Berkshire Chronicle* 6 May 1938 p23 columns 3-5.
[87] This is given as part of the information in Berkshire Record Office,
document reference D/Ex 725/2 "*Burghfield Parish Magazine* 1904 to
1910," in an insert to the March 1907 magazine:
  List of Past and Present Members of the Navy, Army and Reserve Force:
    Willink, Francis A. – 1906 Eton College R.V.
    Willink, George O. W. – 1904 Eton College R.V. Sergeant
    Willink, Henry George – 1875-93 Inns of Court Volunteers. All ranks
  from Private to Captain. Signalling certificates, Aldershot and
  Wellington Barracks. First prize for Fencing (Officers) open to whole
  army 1886.
[88] The results are given in the *London Daily News* 12 January 1877 p6
column 3, listing those who were successful by name.
[89] See the *Oxford Journal* 3 February 1877 p5 column 3.

[90] *Men-at-the Bar* by Joseph Foster, Second Edition, 1885 London, published by Hazell, Watson and Viney, p511. This is available online at https://archive.org accessed January 2017.

[91] Ibid. The reference to *Punch* is based on a comment by Henry in *Memoir of William Williamson Willink* by H. G. Willink (Privately printed 1936) p90.

[92] *In Memoriam* in the *Alpine Journal*, Volume 50 p284.

[93] Ibid.

[94] *The Fell and Rock Climbing Club of the English Lake District* Vol. 8 No. 1, 1928, facing p14.

[95] Listed in the *Morning Post* 14 June 1877 p7 column 5. William Nicholls Willink's entry in *Men-at-the Bar* by Joseph Foster, Second Edition, 1885 London, published by Hazell, Watson and Viney, p511, available online at https://archive.org accessed January 2017, states: ... a student at the Inner Temple 22 May 1872 (then aged 24), called to the bar 13 June 1877. Thus, William had enrolled 5 months before his brother Henry, but was called to the bar 5 months after him.

[96] *Memoir of William Williamson Willink* by H. G. Willink (Privately printed 1936) p82 – 83.

[97] Ibid. p93, 96 – 97.

[98] Marriage reported in the *Leamington Spa Courier* 30 November 1878 p4 column 6 – although it incorrectly stated the date as 23 November; the marriage certificate can be found in the London Metropolitan Archives, St. Luke, Westbourne Park, Westminster, Register of Marriages reference P87/LUK2 Item 005, dated 22 November 1878. This is available in the collection "London, England, Marriages and Banns, 1754-1921" https://ancestry.co.uk accessed January 2017.

[99] *Life of Sir George Nicholls* by H. G. Willink p lxx, in *History of the English Poor Law* by Sir George Nicholls, K.C.B., 1904 Revised edition published by P. S. King, London, edited by H. G. Willink.

[100] The *Birmingham Daily Post* 26 February 1876 p6 column 5.

[101] Presentation address on parchment recording 60 years of service of Henry George Willink, dated 1935, in Birmingham Navigations Collection, University of Salford. There is a listing of the items in this collection at http://www.salford.ac.uk accessed January 2017.

[102] *In Memoriam* in the *Alpine Journal*, Volume 50 p286. Henry remained Vice Chairman of Birmingham Canal Navigations from 1906 until his death in 1938.

[103] *Birmingham Evening Despatch* 26 February 1915 p1 column 3

[104] *Birmingham Daily Post* 28 August 1915 p9 column 1

[105] Birmingham Navigations Collection, University of Salford. There is a listing of the items in this collection at http://www.salford.ac.uk accessed January 2017.

[106] *Memoir of William Williamson Willink* by H. G. Willink (Privately printed 1936) p98 – 99

[107] The Marriage Certificate (General Register Office, District Leighton Buzzard Volume 3b p648) details are:

September Nine 1880 at the Parish Church of Wing:

Henry George Willink age 29 Bachelor Barrister at Law of 3 Hyde Park Street, London, father William Williamson Willink Esq.

Mary Grace Ouvry age 30 Spinster of Wing Vicarage, father Peter Thomas Ouvry Vicar of Wing

Married by Licence by P. T. Ouvry, Vicar.

Witnesses W. W. Willink, Harriet Delamain Ouvry, Frederic Ouvry, H. G. Ouvry, C. J. Phillips

[108] *Bucks Herald* 18 September 1880 p9 columns 3 & 4. Sadly, the article names the groom as Mr. William W. Willink, who was actually of course the father of the groom.

[109] *Luton Times and Advertiser* September 1880 p8 column 5.

[110] *In Memoriam* in the *Alpine Journal*, Volume 50 p284.

[111] *Alpine Journal* 1983 p116.

[112] For the children of George and Harriet Nicholls see Note 31 above.

[113] Address given in *Men-at-the Bar* by Joseph Foster, Second Edition, 1885 London, published by Hazell, Watson and Viney, p511. This is available online at https://archive.org accessed January 2017.

[114] History section of http://royaltournament.org accessed Janary 2017.

[115] *London Daily News* 17 June 1886 p3 column 1.

[116] *Alpine Journal* Volume 54 No. 267 November 1943 p108.

[117] *In Memoriam* in the *Alpine Journal*, Volume 50 p284.

[118] *Reading Mercury* 7 May 1938 p21 columns 5 to 7.

[119] *Derby Mercury* 21 June 1882 p6 column 2.

[120] *Memoir of William Williamson Willink* by H. G. Willink (Privately printed 1936) p3, 99 – 100.

[121] 1881 Census (3 April): Class: RG11; Piece: 16; Folio: 34; Page: 18; Parish: St. John's, Paddington. On this date 3 Hyde Park Street contained:

William W. Willink, Head of Household, aged 72, widower, Secretary Public Works L. Commission

Georgiana E. Nicholls, sister-in-law, aged 65

Henry G. Willink, son visitor, aged 29, married, Barrister at Law in Practice, M. A. Oxford

Mary G. Willink, son's wife, visitor, aged 30

Frederick C. Hubber, Butler, aged 27

Julia Church, Cook, aged 46

Charlotte Haines, Lady's Maid, aged 29

Emma Williams, Housemaid, aged 35

Annie Archer, Kitchenmaid, aged 17

Eleanor Float, Nurse, aged 44

[122] *Morning Post* 15 December 1883 p1 column 1 stated under DEATHS: "Willink, - On the 11th inst., at 3 Hyde-park-street, London, William Williamson Willink, aged seventy-five."

Death date and burial details can be found in *Visitation of England and Wales* Volume 2 Edited by Joseph Jackson Howard and Frederick Arthur Crisp (1894) p50. This can be viewed at https://archive.org accessed January 2017.

[123] *Memoir of William Williamson Willink* by H. G. Willink (Privately printed 1936) p100 – 101.

[124] *Manchester Courier and Lancashire General Advertiser* 11 January 1884 p6 column 6.

[125] John Ouvry Willink born on 9th July 1884. His birth was announced in the *St. James's Gazette* 14 July 1884 p15 column 2 and the *Leighton Buzzard Observer and Linslade Gazette* 15 July 1884 p8 column 6. Both record that although the Willinks lived in Albion Street, the baby was born at "Ford-place, Grays, Essex." This was a country residence associated with the Clark family – Mary's sister Harriet Delamain Ouvry (Harry) had married Gerard Collingwood Clark in 1883, and was herself expecting a child – who would be born in due course at Ford Place (see *Leighton Buzzard Observer and Linslade Gazette* 23 September 1884 p8 column 6). Sadly, this child (Peter Senior Clark) also died in infancy, aged 10 months, one month after John Ouvry Willink (see *Leighton Buzzard Observer and Linslade Gazette* 28 July 1885 p8 column 6).

[126] Death certificate (General Register Office, District Paddington Volume 1a p51) states: "Thirteenth June 1885 29 Albion Street, John Ouvry Willink aged 11 months, son of Henry George Willink Barrister at Law, of Meningitis 10 days." Death reported in *London Evening Standard* p1 column 1. He was buried 17 June 1885 St. Mary's, Acton, Parish Burial record 1885 p170, collection "London, England, Church of England Deaths and Burials, 1813-1980" https://www.ancestry.co.uk accessed January 2017.

[127] *In Memoriam* in the *Alpine Journal*, Volume 50 p285.

[128] *Worcester Chronicle* 27 June 1885 p8 column 6: "Birth – Willink – June 20 at The Halesend, Cradley, Malvern, the wife of W. N. Willink, of a son."

[129] Catharine Dorothy Willink was born 15 October 1885, announced in the *Morning Post* 17 October 1885 p1 column 1. Her birth date is also given in her baptism record, 25 November 1885 available online in collection "London Metropolitan Archives, Paddington St John, Register of Baptism" https://www.ancestry.co.uk accessed January 2017.

[130] In the *Morning Post* 25 January 1886 p8 column 4 there was an advert-

isement for the February 1886 edition of *Longman's Magazine*, Number XL which included the article "Map-flapping. By H. G. Willink. Illustrated." Henry wrote a follow-up article for the March 1886 edition – "Map-flapping (Solution of a Problem)" – advertised in the *Pall Mall Gazette* 24 February 1886 p14 column 2. There is a brief description of the methods used, with diagrams, in the *Illustrated London News* 20 March 1886 pages 13 and 14.

[131] From *The Hemel Hempstead Gazette* 23 January 1886 p8 column 4.

[132] *Exeter and Plymouth Gazette* 5 April 1886 p4 column 5.

[133] *London Evening Standard* 13 November 1886 p3 column 2.

[134] George Ouvry William Willink was born on 1 February 1888 at 1 Hyde Park Street, Paddington – announced in the *Leighton Buzzard Observer and Linslade Gazette* 7 February 1888 p8 column 6. He was baptised 3 March 1888 – the Parish Baptism record is in collection "London Metropolitan Archives, Paddington St John, Register of Baptism" https://www.ancestry.co.uk accessed January 2017.

[135] *The Fell and Rock Climbing Club of the English Lake District* Vol. 8 No. 1 1928 p16.

[136] *The Graphic* 28 September 1889 article p400, 402; sketches p376f.

[137] *Worcester Journal* 2 March 1889 p3 column 1.

[138] William Nicholls Willink died 9 April 1891 at Farndon, Newark-on-Trent. *Worcestershire Chronicle* 18 April 1891 p4 column 7.

[139] *Glasgow Herald* 23 November 1889 p3 column 1.

[140] *The London Gazette* 3 January 1890 p10 column 2.

[141] *London Evening Standard* 31 March 1890 p5 column 3 & p6 column 3.

[142] *Leighton Buzzard Observer and Linslade Gazette* 4 February 1890 p1 column 4.

[143] Ibid. 18 February 1890 p5 column 5.

[144] A few references to lectures on mountaineering by way of example:

"Mountaineering" at the Royal Victoria Hall, London on 28 October 1890 (*London Daily News* 28 October 1890 p2 column 3);

"Snow Mountains" at the Royal Victoria Hall on 5 December 1893 (*Morning Post* 4 December 1893 p5 column 5);

"Alpine Climbing" to the Working Men's College, Great Ormond Street on 4 December 1897 (*Morning Post* 24 September 1897 p2 column 4);

"Mountains" at the Leighton Institute on 4 November 1897 (*Leighton Buzzard and Linslade Gazette* 5 October 1897 p1 column 4 and detailed report 9 November 1897 p5 column 5);

"Alpine Climbing – How not to do it" to the Working Men's College, Great Ormond Street on 13 November 1897 (*London Daily News* 15 November 1897 p6 column 6);

"Climbing in the High Alps" at St. James' Hall, Lichfield, on 8 February

1900 (*Lichfield Mercury* 9 February 1900 p5 column 3);
    "Snow Mountains" in Burghfield on 16 January 1903 (*Reading Mercury* 24 January 1903 p3 column 2).

[145] *In Memoriam* in the *Alpine Journal*, Volume 50 p285.

[146] Ibid. Also see *Memoir of William Williamson Willink* by H. G. Willink (Privately printed 1936) p57.

[147] The grounds were described in an advertisement in the *Morning Post* 17 July 1888 p8 column 1. Details of the architect are given on www.heritagegateway.org.uk Historic Environment Record Number MWB16811 accessed January 2017.

[148] *Reading Mercury* 26 May 1888 p5 column 4.

[149] Catalogue of Household Furniture for Highwoods, Burghfield Hill; sale dates 26th, 27th & 28th November 1889. This catalogue can be found in the Local Studies section of Reading Central Library. There is also a description of the house and grounds in *Jackson's Oxford Journal* 1 June 1889 p4 column 5.

[150] *Reading Mercury* 9 November 1889 p4 column 6.

[151] The date is given in HGW's handwriting in the front inside cover of his bound copies of *Burghfield Parish Magazines* for 1889-1903 now held at Berkshire Record Office, document reference D/EX 725/1.

[152] Francis Arthur Willink born 14 February 1891 at Highwoods – *Leighton Buzzard Observer and Linslade Gazette* 17 February 1891 p8 column 6. For his baptism see Berkshire Record Office, document reference D/P 29/1/7 "Baptisms, Burghfield Parish Register 1838-1913," also D/EX 725/1 "*Burghfield Parish Magazines* 1889-1903," May 1891.

[153] *Pall Mall Gazette* 27 June 1890 p3 column 3.

[154] *Dundee Courier* 28 June 1890 p6 column 1.

[155] *The Scots Magazine* 1 September 1890 p302.

[156] 1891 Census (5 April): Class: RG12; Piece: 990; Folio: 53; Page: 10; Parish: Burghfield.

[157] *Crockford's Clerical Directory*, London 1898 p594. For his starting date at Burghfield, see *Guernsey Star* 18 November 1879 p2 column 3 which carried news of the preferment to the living. For his retirement see *Reading Mercury* 3 June 1911 p6 column 6.

[158] 1911 census reference: Class: RG14; Piece: 6547; Schedule Number: 204. Florence Harington died 4 April 1884 – *London Evening Standard* 7 April 1884 p1 column 1. Florence's parents were also living at the Rectory according to the censuses of 1881 and 1891. 1881 census reference: Class: RG11; Piece: 1298; Folio 37; Page: 12. 1891 census reference: Class: RG12; Piece: 990; Folio: 40; Page: 14.

[159] Berkshire Record Office, document reference D/EX 725/1 "*Burghfield Parish Magazine* 1889 – 1903," February 1891 p2.

[160] Ibid. May 1891 p3.

[161] For the death of William Nicholls Willink, see Note 136 above. His Probate record can be viewed in collection "England & Wales National Probate Calendar (Index of Wills and Administrations), 1858-1966" for 1891 https://www.ancestry.co.uk accessed January 2017. His son Thomas Wingfield Willink stated that his uncle, Henry, was his next of kin on his army registration papers.

[162] This can be seen at http://southwellchurches.nottingham.ac.uk/farndon accessed January 2017.

[163] Obituary of Thomas Bland Garland in the *Minutes of the Proceedings of the Institute of Civil Engineers*, Volume 109 (1892) pages 426-428.

[164] Marriage of Horatio Bland and Emily Alicia Cherry on 3 August 1847 – see *London Standard* 5 August 1847 p4 column 6. For their residence at Culverlands see 1851 England Census Class: HO107; Piece: 1691; Folio: 372; Page: 18. The date of the building of Hillfields is taken from a date plaque on one of its chimneys.

Emily Alicia Bland died on 16 March 1868 and was buried in Jerusalem's Protestant Cemetery – see http://findagrave.com accessed January 2017.

[165] Horatio Bland died 31 March 1876 "At the Bungalow, Burghfield," *Hampshire Advertiser* 5 April 1876 p2 column 1.

[166] *Reading Mercury* 4 June 1892 p3 column 4.

[167] Berkshire Record Office, document reference RD/B Ca 1/1 "Bradfield Rural District Council 1888 – 1895" p171.

[168] Ibid. passim.

[169] *In Memoriam* in the *Alpine Journal*, Volume 50 p284-285.

[170] *Alpine Journal* Volume 27 p62.

[171] *Pall Mall Gazette* 19 July 1892 p3 column 1.

[172] Berkshire Record Office, document reference D/EX 725/1 "*Burghfield Parish Magazine* 1889 – 1903," September 1891 p2.

[173] Ibid. November 1891 p2.

[174] *Reading Mercury* 6 February 1892 p5 column 5.

[175] Ibid. 13 February 1892 p6 column 3.

[176] Sanitary Authority of Bradfield Union – Berkshire Record Office, document reference RD/B Ca 1/1 "Bradfield Rural District Council 1888 – 1895" meeting of 19 April 1892. Guardians of the Bradfield Union – Berkshire Record Office, document reference G/B 1/27 meeting of 19 April 1892.

[177] *Reading Mercury* 16 April 1892 p4 column 1.

[178] Ibid. 25 June 1892 p8 column 4.

[179] Berkshire Record Office, document reference D/EX 1940/1 "Sale Catalogue for Hillfields." The sale was originally scheduled for 30 June, but took place on 15 July.

[180] *Reading Mercury* 4 June 1892 p3 column 4.

[181] *In Memoriam* of Clinton Thomas Dent by H. G. Willink, *Alpine Journal* Volume 27 p61-62; the operation is also mentioned in *In Memoriam* of Henry George Willink, *Alpine Journal* Volume 50 p285 written by Henry's daughter Katie.

[182] *Reading Mercury* 24 December 1892 p2 column 6. The Reading Savings Bank Annual General Meeting was held on Tuesday 20 December 1892.

[183] *The National Magazine and Monthly Critic*, No. 1, August 1837, published in London by W. Edwards, p101-102.

[184] *Reading Mercury* 24 December 1892 p7 columns 5 & 6.

[185] Trustee Savings Banks in the UK 1810-1995 at http://savings-banks.com accessed January 2017.

[186] *Reading Mercury* 8 April 1893 p5 column 2.

[187] Ibid. p2 column 1.

[188] Ibid. 15 April 1893 p5 column 3.

[189] From the author's collection

[190] *Lichfield Mercury* 27 February 1891 p4 column 3 – an advertisement for a talk by Henry to the Lichfield Charity Organization Society.

[191] *The Dutch Home Labour Colonies: their Origins and Development* by H. G. Willink, published by Kegan Paul, Trench & Co. 1889. This was a compilation of Henry's papers to the *Charity Organization Review*.

[192] *Morning Post* 13 May 1889 p8 column 3

[193] Berkshire Record Office, document reference D/Ex 374/5.

[194] *Lichfield Mercury* 6 March 1891 p8 columns 1 & 2.

[195] *Report of the Proceedings of the 22nd Annual Poor Law Conference for the West Midland District held at the Imperial Hotel, Malvern, on May 5th & 6th 1891* published by Knight & Co. London. A copy of this paper can be found at Berkshire Record Office in a blue bound book on their library shelves entitled *Pamphlets: Poor Law, Charity, etc*. This book belonged previously to Henry, as shown by his signature on the flyleaf. He had this collection of miscellaneous Poor Law papers bound.

[196] Ibid. p10. Also reported in *Gloucestershire Chronicle* 9 May 1891 p3 column 6.

[197] Berkshire Record Office, document reference G/B 1/26 "Meetings of the Guardians of the Bradfield Union March 1888 to November 1891." Henry's first attendance was Tuesday 19 May 1891.

[198] *Reading Mercury* 30 January 1892 p2 column 4. The meeting took place at Highwoods.

[199] Ibid. 23 April 1892 p4 column 1.

[200] *Leighton Buzzard Observer and Linslade Gazette* 17 January 1893 p5 columns 3 to 6.

[201] *Reading Mercury* 12 August 1893 p5 column 3; report of the conference and Henry's speech in *Reading Mercury* 28 October 1893 p6 column 1.

[202] *London Standard* 8 November 1893 p3 column 6.

[203] Berkshire Record Office, document reference G/B 1/27 "Meetings of the Guardians of the Bradfield Union 1891 to 1895" and RD/B/CA 1/1 "Meetings of the Sanitary Authority of the Bradfield Union 1888 to 1895."

[204] Berkshire Record Office, document reference G/B 1/27 "Meetings of the Guardians of the Bradfield Union 1891 to 1895."

[205] *Reading Mercury* 7 December 1895 p2 column 2.

[206] Following his paper of October 1893 (see Note 192 above), Henry's papers included:

"The Parish Councils Act" November 1894 – pamphlet quoted in full in Berkshire Record Office, document reference D/EX 725/1 "*B*s 1889 – 1903" December 1894 p2 and 3;

"Parochial self-government in rural districts" in the *Charity Organization Society Review* June 1894.

"A Spirit of Enterprise" to the Charity Organization Annual Conference in Cheltenham on 29 April 1895 – see reports in *Cheltenham Chronicle* 4 May 1895 p3 columns 1 to 3 and *Reading Mercury* 4 May 1895 p5 column 3;

"The Principles of the English Poor Law" to the Central Poor Law Conference on 4 March 1896 – see *Morning Post* 5 March 1896 p6 column 7 and *Western Times* 11 March 1896 p3 column 4;

"The Outdoor Relief Question" (read by C. T. Dent) to the West London Charity Organization Society Conference on 30 November 1897 – see *London Evening Standard* 1 December 1897 p8 column 5;

"The Treatment of Infectious Diseases in Country Districts, and particularly in relation to the Poor Law" on 10 December 1897 to the South-Eastern Poor Law Conference – see *Morning Post* 11 December 1897 p6 column 1;

"By-Laws (Buildings and Others) in Rural Districts" on 6 December 1900 to the South-Eastern and Metropolitan Poor Law Conference – see *London Daily News* 7 December 1900 p5 column 4 and *Reading Mercury* 15 December 1900 p9 column 1;

"Relief by Way of Loan with special reference to Medical Relief" on 26 May 1902 to the Society of Poor Law Workers;

"Medical Relief" on 29 May 1903 to the South Midland Poor Law Conference – see *Buckingham Advertiser and Free Press* 30 May 1903 p5 column 3 and *Bucks Herald* 6 June 1903 p2 column 5;

"Forming Voluntary Relief Committees" on 9 October 1907 to the South-West Poor Law Conference – see *Western Daily Press* 10 October 1907 p7 column 4.

Most of these papers can be found at Berkshire Record Office in blue bound books on their library shelves variously entitled *Pamphlets: Poor Law, Charity, etc* of various dates. These books belonged previously to Henry, as shown by his signature on the flyleaf. He had this collection of miscellaneous Poor Law papers bound in several volumes.

[207] *London Daily News* 11 May 1898 p8 column 5.

[208] Berkshire Record Office, document reference D/EX 1940/1 "Catalogue 1892 Sale of Hillfields."

[209] *Reading Mercury* 21 October 1893 p5 column 7; Berkshire Record Office, document reference D/EX 725/1 "*Burghfield Parish Magazine 1889 – 1903*" November 1893 p3.

[210] *Lakeland Memories in The Fell and Rock Climbing Club of the English Lake District* Vol. 8 No. 1 1928 p17.

[211] *Badminton Library Big Game Shooting* Volume 1 by C. Phillipps-Wolley published by Longmans, Green & Co., London 1894 – vignettes on p27 and 475. Advertised *London Evening Standard* 28 February 1894 p4 column 1. The whole text can be found at https://archive.org accessed January 2017.

[212] Annual meeting 18 July 1892 – see *Reading Mercury* 23 July 1892 p5 column 4 and Berkshire Record Office, document reference D/EX 725/1 "*Burghfield Parish Magazines* 1889 – 1903" August 1892 p3.

Annual meeting 10 July 1893 - see *Reading Mercury* 15 July 1893 p4 column 3 and Berkshire Record Office, document reference D/EX 725/1 "*Burghfield Parish Magazines* 1889 – 1903" August 1893 p3.

Annual meeting 16 July 1894 – see *Reading Mercury* 21 July 1894 p5 column 5.

Henry's sketchbooks (in the possession of Janet and Duncan Davies) show that he was on holiday in Italy at the time of the 1892 meeting.

[213] Berkshire Record Office, document reference D/EX 752/2 "*Burghfield Parish Magazine* 1904 – 1910" December 1910 p3.

[214] Berkshire Record Office, document reference D/EX 752/8 "*Burghfield Parish Magazine* 1935 – 1936" December 1936 p3.

[215] *Reading Mercury* 3 March 1894 p4 column 4 and 28 July 1894 p1 column 3 (although the latter incorrectly calls the property Highfields – a cross between Highwoods and Hillfields, perhaps?).

[216] *Reading Mercury* 14 October 1893 p6 column 4.

[217] Berkshire Record Office, document reference D/EX 725/1 "*Burghfield Parish Magazines* 1889 – 1903" October 1896 p2 and 3.

[218] *Reading Mercury* 11 August 1894 p7 column 1.

[219] The Portman Club first visited Burghfield at Henry's invitation in 1892. References to their visits can be found at Berkshire Record Office, document reference D/EX 725/1 "*Burghfield Parish Magazines* 1889 –

1903" October 1896 p2 and 3; *Reading Mercury* 17 July 1897 p3 column 1, 16 July 1898 p4 column 4, 22 July 1899 p3 column 3, 21 July 1900 p3 column 4, 12 July 1902 p7 column 4, and 15 July 1905 p6 column 4.

[220] *Reading Mercury* 13 July 1895 p5 column 5.

[221] Ibid. 5 October 1895 p8 column 5 and Berkshire Record Office, document reference D/EX 725/1 "*Burghfield Parish Magazines* 1889 – 1903" August 1895 p2, August 1896 p2 to 3.

[222] *Reading Mercury* 15 December 1894 p5 column 7 and 22 December 1894 p6 column 2.

[223] Berkshire Record Office, document reference RD/B/CA 1/1 "Meetings of the Sanitary Authority of the Bradfield Union 1888 to 1895."

[224] *Reading Mercury* 12 January 1895 p4 column 2; also Berkshire Record Office, document reference D/EX 725/1 "*Burghfield Parish Magazines* 1889 – 1903" February 1895 p2. Henry stood down as chairman a year later – see Henry's hand written note in Berkshire Record Office, document reference D/EX 725/1 "*Burghfield Parish Magazines* 1889 – 1903" April 1896.

[225] *Reynold's Newspaper* 14 June 1896 p3 column 3. Articles on the book can be found in *The Graphic* 27 June 1896 p774 and *The Standard* 26 June 1896 p2 columns 4 and 5.

[226] The *Badminton Magazine* article was advertised in the *Pall Mall Gazette* 2 August 1895 p5 column 3. A review of the watercolours at the annual Newbury Exhibition can be found in *Reading Mercury* 17 December 1892 p2 columns 1 & 2, 27 October 1894 p4 column 3; 19 October 1895 p2 columns 4 & 5 – in this report their paintings are identified: Henry – "Oxford on the Alde", Mary – "Fishing Boats;" 16 October 1897 p3 column 2 – here it states "Mr. Willink's waves are very good."

[227] *Reading Mercury* 31 August 1895 p2 columns 1 & 2, and 2 September 1899 p3 columns 1 & 2.

[228] Ibid. 13 March 1897 p2 column 4.

[229] Ibid. 12 June 1897 p2 columns 1 to 4.

[230] Ibid. 9 December 1899 p3 columns 1 to 3.

[231] Ibid. 3 July 1897 p2 column 4.

[232] Ibid. 5 February 1898 p6 column 3; also Berkshire Record Office, document reference D/EX 725/1 "*Burghfield Parish Magazines* 1889 – 1903" March 1898 p2 and 3. William Edward Willink was the son of William Williamson Willink's brother Arthur.

[233] The first lecture is noted in *Reading Mercury* 5 February 1898 p6 column 3. The fourth and final one is reported in *Reading Mercury* 26 February 1898 p7 column 7.

[234] Berkshire Record Office, document reference D/EX 725/1 "*Burghfield Parish Magazines* 1889 – 1903" April 1899 p2.

[235] Berkshire Record Office, document reference RB/B Ca 1/2 "Minutes of Bradfield Rural District Council 1895 – 1900" meetings of 1 July 1899 and 8 August 1899.

[236] Henry was elected onto the committee of the Royal Berkshire Friendly Society at the Annual Meeting on 16 April 1898, reported in the *Berkshire Chronicle* 23 April 1898 p2 columns 3 and 4. He had previously attended at least one of their annual meetings – see *Reading Mercury* 22 April 1893 p2 column 5. He was re-elected on the committee annually up to 1911-12 – see *Reading Mercury* 22 April 1911 p9 column 6. He was not on the committee from 1914-15 – *Reading Mercury* 25 April 1914 p10 columns 1 and 2.

[237] *Reading Mercury* 20 July 1895 p4 column 2.

[238] Ibid. 29 September 1900 p6 column 2.

[239] Information about Henry's membership of the Alpine Club is from *In Memoriam* in the *Alpine Journal*, Volume 50 p284. Regarding Henry's visit to Switzerland, see *Reading Mercury* 20 July 1901 p4 column 4. This article describes the 35th Anniversary Fete of the Oddfellows at Hillfields, in spite of their host and Honorary Treasurer's absence abroad. The visit to Great Sugar Loaf is given in Berkshire Record Office, document reference D/EX 725/1 "*Burghfield Parish Magazines* 1889 – 1903." Henry has annotated a photograph of "Bantry Bay and the Great Sugar Loaf Mountain" in the Sulhamstead Parish magazine for August 1901: "George and I went up Sugar Loaf alone together 2/9/00 from Glengariff."

[240] 1901 Census (31 March): Class: RG13; Piece: 1106; Folio: 112; Page: 17; Parish: Eversley, Hampshire. This record gives George (aged 13) and Francis (aged 10) as pupils of St. Neot's School.

[241] The Confirmation service was reported in the *Reading Mercury* 22 February 1902 p6 column 3. In the collection of *Burghfield Parish Magazines* at Berkshire Record Office, document reference D/EX 725/1, there is an entry for March 1902 that gives Catharine's name as one of the candidates and Henry has added a hand-written note about their travel to Rome.

[242] *Reading Mercury* 16 August 1902 p4 column 1.

[243] Berkshire Record Office, document reference D/EX 725/1 "*Burghfield Parish Magazines* 1889 – 1903" September 1902 p3.

[244] *Reading Mercury* 16 April 1892 p4 column 1, being a report of the Vestry meeting at St. Mary's, Burghfield.

[245] Ibid. 30 April 1898 p6 column 5.

[246] Ibid. 30 May 1903 p2 column 1.

[247] Berkshire Record Office, document reference C/CL C4/3/1 "Minutes of the Berkshire Education Committee Volume 1 June 1903 – October 1905."

[248] Ibid.

[249] Ibid.

[250] Ibid. meeting of 15 April 1905. Examples of these medals can be seen at Berkshire Record Office, document reference D/EX 603/1, D/EX 1166/1 and D/EX 1201/1.

[251] Berkshire Record Office, document reference D/EX 725/2 "*Burghfield Parish Magazines* 1904 – 1910" March 1906 p2.

[252] Information from the online Berkshire Record Office catalogue for document reference D/EX 603/1.

[253] *Berkshire Chronicle* 28 April 1906 p3 column 4.

[254] *Reading Mercury* 25 March 1939 p3 column 5.

[255] Election as Chairman of the Berkshire Education Committee: *Berkshire Chronicle* 29 April 1908 p3 column 2. For his resignation from the position, see Berkshire Record Office, document reference D/EX 725/7 "*Burghfield Parish Magazine* 1931 – 1934" for June 1932.

[256] *Reading Mercury* 11 February 1905 p5 column 2.

[257] Ibid. 11 March 1905 p6 column 1.

[258] Ibid. 18 March 1905 p2 columns 1 and 2.

[259] *Berkshire Chronicle* 14 October 1905 p8 column 4.

[260] *Reading Mercury* 27 May 1905 p4 column 1 and 3 June 1905 p9 column 5.

[261] *Berkshire Chronicle* 24 September 1892 p8 column 4.

[262] *Times* 5 May 1938 Issue 47986 p18 column C; *Berkshire Chronicle* 6 May 1938 p23 columns 3 to 5. The Reading University Charter of Incorporation is downloadable from www.reading.ac.uk accessed Janaury 2017.

[263] Henry's sketchbooks in the possession of Janet and Duncan Davies, and *In Memoriam* in the *Alpine Journal*, Volume 50 p285.

[264] Berkshire Record Office, document D/EX 725/2 *Burghfield Parish Magazines* 1904 – 1910 for May 1908. Hand-written note by Henry.

[265] Collection "UK Outward Passenger Lists 1890 – 1960" https://www.ancestry.co.uk accessed January 2017.

[266] Collection "New York Passenger Lists 1820 – 1957" https://www.ancestry.co.uk accessed January 2017. The snow storm is mentioned on a sketch by Henry, "Approach to New York," in a sketchbook owned by Janet and Duncan Davies.

[267] Berkshire Record Office, document reference D/EX 725/2 "*Burghfield Parish Magazines* 1904 – 1910" May 1910 p3; also *Reading Mercury* 23 April 1910 p3 column 6.

[268] Berkshire Record Office, document reference D/EX 725/1 "*Burghfield Parish Magazine* 1889 – 1903" for July 1901, and D/EX 725/3 "*Burghfield Parish Magazine* 1911 – 1916" for July 1912.

[269] 1911 census (2 April) Class: RG14; Piece: 6547; Schedule Number: 69.

[270] *In Memoriam* of Clinton Thomas Dent by H. G. Willink, *Alpine Journal* Volume 27 p65.

[271] Details of holidays are from Henry's sketchbooks which are in the possession of Janet and Duncan Davies. The voyage to Colombo can be found in the collection "UK Outward Passenger Lists 1890 – 1960" https://www.ancestry.co.uk accessed January 2017. The original Passenger Manifest gives Miss Grace Willink, but this is an error for Katie.

[272] *Reading Mercury* 15 February 1913 p2 column 1.

[273] Details are from Henry's sketchbooks which are in the possession of Janet and Duncan Davies. The voyage to Marseilles can be found in the collection "UK Outward Passenger Lists 1890 – 1960" https://www.ancestry.co.uk accessed January 2017.

[274] With thanks to Janet and Duncan Davies for Pilkington family history details.

[275] *Reading Mercury* 31 January 1914 p8 column 2; also see Berkshire Record Office, document reference D/EX 725/3 "*Burghfield Parish Magazines* 1911 – 1916" for February 1914.

[276] *Reading Mercury* 28 March 1914 p4 column 4.

[277] With thanks to Mr. Bozi Mohacek, Chairman of Surrey Vintage Vehicle Society, for details of the car and its registration.

[278] George Ouvry William Willink as Second Lieutenant in the Inns of Court OTC – see *London Gazette* 15 April 1913 Issue 28710 p2728 column 1. Francis Arthur Willink's degree details – see *Birmingham Daily Post* 30 Jun 1914 p6 column 7. As Lieutenant in the Territorial Force, Royal Berkshire Regiment – see *London Gazette* 5 August 1913 Issue 28743 p5574 column 2.

[279] *Reading Mercury* 22 August 1914 p3 column 3; Berkshire Record Office, document reference D/EX 725/3 "*Burghfield Parish Magazines* 1911 – 1916" for September 1914. This latter reference includes a long article by Henry explaining why Britain was at war and what the requirements were for joining the Army.

[280] Berkshire Record Office, document reference D/EX 725/3 "*Burghfield Parish Magazines* 1911 – 1916" for October 1914.

[281] *Reading Mercury* 26 December 1914 p5 column 7: "Births: PILKINGTON- On the 17th inst., at Hillfields, Burghfield, the wife of Edward F. Pilkington, Captain 6th (1st Reserve) Battalion Manchester Regiment, of Ingleside, Irlams-o,-th'-Height, Manchester, of a daughter."

[282] Berkshire Record Office, document reference D/EX 725/3 "*Burghfield Parish Magazine* 1911 – 1916" entries for November and December 1914. The Laurent family are named in Henry's photo album for 1914 to 1923, in the possession of Janet and Duncan Davies.

[283] *Reading Mercury* 29 August 1914 p6 column 2 and 19 June 1915 p5 column 7.

[284] Berkshire Record Office, document reference C/CL C1/1/18 "Berkshire

County Council Minutes" 16 October 1915.
[285] *Reading Mercury* 22 August 1914 p3 column 3 and 9 October 1915 p3 column 3.
[286] The Tribunals were often reported in the *Reading Mercury* in detail. For example, see 1 April 1916 p8 column 4.
[287] Henry's involvement included being:
Chairman of the Bradfield Rural District Council (monthly meeting);
Member of the following Sub-committees:

- Highways
- Finance
- General Purposes – chaired by Henry
- Sewerage and Waterworks – chaired by Henry
- Procedure
- Contracts
- Bye-Laws
- War Agricultural Committee

Guardian of the Poor of Bradfield Union (monthly meeting)
Member of the following Sub-committees:

- Assessment
- House
- Finance
- Children Act
- Boarding-Out
- Joint Relief

Chairman of the Berkshire Education Committee (Quarterly main meeting)
Member of the following Sub-committees:

- Higher Education
- School Management
- Works
- By-Laws and School Attendance
    - Bradfield Rural District School Attendance Local Sub-committee
- Education Finance
- War Savings (Education) – chaired by Henry
- Cadet Training

Berkshire County Council Alderman (Quarterly main meeting)
Member of the following Sub-committees:

- Assessment and County Boundaries
- Finance and General Purposes

183

- Joint Sanatorium
- Berkshire Agricultural Instruction

Representative of the BCC on the County Councils' Association

Berkshire County Council's War Agricultural Committee

Chairman of the Bradfield Tribunal (weekly meeting)

Berkshire National Relief Fund Committee

Governor of:

- Reading School,
- Maidenhead Boys' School and
- Maidenhead Girls' School

Member of the University College Council and Life Governor

Justice of the Peace

- County Bench (approx. monthly)
- Berkshire Quarterly Assizes,
- Lunacy committee

Church warden at St Mary's, Burghfield

Lay Member of Oxford Diocesan Council

Birmingham Canal Navigations Vice Chairman (monthly)

Captain in Command, No. 8 Company of the 1st Battalion, Berkshire National Reserve

This list is almost certainly not complete!

[288] There is a note in Henry's photograph album stating that he went to bed on 11 October for 10 weeks and Mary on 20 October for 8 weeks. He calls it "A Bad Time." Henry is also recorded as absent in the minutes of his many committees until 30 December, when he was present at a Berkshire County Council meeting.

[289] Honor Pilkington's birth reference is Date: Jan/Mar 1917; District: Bradfield; Volume:2c; Page: 540.

[290] Berkshire Record Office, document reference G/B 1/37 "Minutes of the Board of Guardians of the Poor of Bradfield Union 1917 – 1918," meeting of 17 April 1917. Also see RB/B CA 1/12 "Minutes of Bradfield Rural District Council 1917 – 1918," meeting of 17 April 1917.

[291] *London Gazette* 15 September 1914 Issue 28902 p7308 column 2 and 20 June 1916 Issue 29633 p6199 column 2.

[292] Ibid. 7 September 1915 Supplement 29289 p8983 column 1.

[293] Ibid. 19 June 1917 Issue 30139 p6123 column 1.

[294] Berkshire Record Office, document reference D/EX 725/4 "*Burghfield Parish Magazines* 1917 – 1921" October 1917 p3.

[295] *Reading Mercury* 27 October 1917 p2 column 5.

[296] Berkshire Record Office, document reference D/EX 725/4 "*Burghfield Parish Magazines* 1917 – 1921" December 1917 p3.

[297] Details are from Henry's photograph album which is in the possession of Janet and Duncan Davies.

[298] Death certificate Quarter Jan-Mar 1918; District: Bradfield; Volume 2c; page 478. Mary's death was announced in the *Reading Mercury* 16 February 1918 p5 column 7.

[299] *Reading Mercury* 16 February 1918 p7 col 3.

[300] Berkshire Record Office, document reference D/EX 725/4 "*Burghfield Parish Magazines* 1917 – 1921" March 1918.

[301] *Reading Mercury* 5 October 1918 p4 column 3. Also see Berkshire Record Office, document reference D/EX 725/4 "*Burghfield Parish Magazines* 1917 – 1921" April 1919.

[302] *Reading Mercury* 13 April 1918 p5 column 5.

[303] Ibid. 27 April 1918 p5 column 7.

[304] *The Newsletter of the Western Front Association*, Thames Valley Branch Number 31, December 2012, pages 6 to 8.

[305] *Reading Mercury* 27 April 1918 p2 columns 3 & 4; Berkshire Record Office, document reference D/EX 725/4 "*Burghfield Parish Magazines* 1917 – 1921" July 1918.

[306] His grave is reference XVII.F.9. See entry in the Commonwealth War Graves Commission website www.cwgc.org accessed January 2017.

[307] Berkshire Record Office, document reference D/EX 725/4 "*Burghfield Parish Magazines* 1917 – 1921" June 1918.

[308] *London Gazette* 31 May 1918 Supplement 30712 p6356 column 2.

[309] *Reading Mercury* 16 November 1918 p3 column 5.

[310] Ibid. 2 August 1919 p9 column 4.

[311] Berkshire Record Office, document reference D/EX 725/4 "*Burghfield Parish Magazines* 1917 – 1921" December 1920 and February 1921.

[312] Charles Pilkington's birth reference is Date: Jan/Mar 1921; District: Salford; Volume:8d; Page: 59.

[313] Edward Michael Pilkington's birth reference is Date: Apr/Jun 1924; District: Salford; Volume:8d; Page: 39.

[314] Hester Anita Clark married Leonard Maurice Edward Dent at St. John's Church, Paddington, on 6 July 1920. The marriage certificate can be viewed in collection "London, England, Marriages and Banns 1754 – 1921" https://www.ancestry.co.uk accessed January 2017.

[315] These details are from information in Henry's photograph album for 1914 – 1923, in the possession of Janet and Duncan Davies.

[316] Berkshire Record Office, document reference D/EX 725/4 "*Burghfield Parish Magazines* 1917 – 1921" August and September 1921.

[317] Berkshire Record Office, document reference D/EX 725/5 "*Burghfield Parish Magazines* 1922 – 1925" June 1924.

[318] Berkshire Record Office, document reference D/EX 725/4 "*Burghfield*

Parish Magazines 1917 – 1921." Elected onto the PCC – see May 1920; PCC Secretary and Treasurer – see June 1921; other roles – see December 1921.

[319] Berkshire Record Office, document reference D/EX 725/5 "*Burghfield Parish Magazines* 1922 – 1925" September 1923.

[320] Ibid. September 1925.

[321] *The Fell and Rock Climbing Club of the English Lake District* Vol. 8 No. 1 1928 p17 – 18.

[322] Berkshire Record Office, document reference D/EX 725/6 "*Burghfield Parish Magazines* 1926 – 1930" June 1926.

[323] Ibid. June 1930.

[324] Berkshire Record Office, document reference D/EX 725/7 "*Burghfield Parish Magazines* 1931 – 1934" April 1932.

[325] Berkshire Record Office, document reference C/CL C4/3/15 "Minutes of Berkshire Education Committee 1932 to 1933."

[326] Berkshire Record Office, document reference D/EX 725/7 "*Burghfield Parish Magazines* 1931 – 1934" June 1932.

[327] Ibid. October 1932; also see Berkshire Record Office, document reference C/CL C4/3/15 "Minutes of Berkshire Education Committee 1932 – 1933."

[328] *In Memoriam* in the *Alpine Journal*, Volume 50 p285.

[329] Berkshire Record Office, document reference D/EX 725/8 "*Burghfield Parish Magazines* 1935 – 1936" December 1936.

[330] Berkshire Record Office, document reference C/CL C4/3/18 "Minutes of Berkshire Education Committee 1938 – 1939."

[331] *Reading Mercury* 7 May 1938 columns 5 to 7.

[332] Ibid.

[333] Death certificate Apr/Jun 1938; Sub-district: Bradfield; Volume 2c; page 469.

[334] Revised Standard Version (1901) Apocrypha

[335] Obituaries can be found in *Reading Mercury* 7 May 1938 columns 5 to 7, *Berkshire Chronicle* 6 May 1938 p23 col 3-5, and *The Times* 5 May 1938 Issue 47986 p18 col C.

[336] *Berkshire Chronicle* 29 July 1938 p15 column 1. The value of Henry's estate was originally calculated to be £87,085 10s 11d, but was "reworn" to be the amount given in the text. See Collection "England & Wales National Probate Calendar (Index of Wills and Administrations) 1858-1966 for 1938" https://ancestry.co.uk accessed January 2017.

[337] *Antique Collector* August/September 1964 p135. Also see the obituary of Major Leonard Dent in *The Times* 24 July 1987.

[338] *Antique Collector* August/September 1964 p135.

[339] *History of Guide Dogs* available at www.guidedogs.org.uk accessed January 2017.

List of Illustrations

Abbreviations used:

Badminton	*The Badminton Library: Mountaineering* by C. T. Dent, 1892 London, published by Longmans, Green & Co. – In the author's collection
Fencing	*Fencing* by H. A. Colmore Dunn, 1906 London, published by George Bell & Sons – In the author's collection
Photograph - F	Photograph in possession of the family and used with permission
Photograph – MS	Photograph by the author, or in the author's collection
Poor Law	*History of the English Poor Law* by Sir George Nicholls, K.C.B., 1904 Revised edition published by P. S. King, London - In the author's collection
Sketchbook	From one of H. G. Willink's sketchbooks, in possession of the family and used with permission
Snap	*Snap: A Legend of the Lone Mountain* by C. Phillipps-Wolley, 1890 London, published by Longmans, Green & Co. – In the author's collection

A Biography of H. G. Willink 1851 – 1938

Illustrations:

	Page
Henry George Willink, aged 50 (Photograph - F)	viii
Initial I – A Glass I (Badminton p402)	ix
William Williamson Willink (*Memoir of William Williamson Willink* by H. G. Willink (Privately printed 1836) Frontispiece, in the family's possession and used with permission)	x
Initial H – A chamber scene (Badminton p75)	1
Catharine Harriet Willink (Painting in the family's possession and used with permission)	2
Willink shield (Photograph – MS)	3
Willink/Ouvry crest (Photograph – MS)	4
The Willink School crest	4
Princess of Orange's Jewel (Photograph - F)	7
Early drawing by Henry, 1855 (Sketchbook)	12
No. 3 Hyde Park Street (Photograph - F)	13
Sketch of Eton College, 1907 (Sketchbook)	14
Initial S – Stonecrop (Badminton p380)	15
Gunterstein (Sketchbook)	20
Wilderwurm Gletscher (Badminton p19)	23
On the Messer Grat (Badminton p204)	24
Willy on Cader Idris, 1878 (Sketchbook)	28
Initial R – Alpenrose (Badminton p xvii)	29
No. 1: Hallo – here's a b… (Sketchbook)	32
No.2: …g (Sketchbook)	33
Pillar Rock, the Great Chimney (Sketchbook)	34
Millwall Docks (Sketchbook)	36
Stockholm, Sweden (Sketchbook)	36
Lapp Hut near Skalstugan, Sweden (Sketchbook)	37
Head of Nordfjord, Norway (Sketchbook)	37
The top of the Matterhorn (Sketchbook)	41
Mary Grace Ouvry at the organ, 1876 (Sketchbook)	44
John Ouvry Willink, 1884 (Sketchbook)	48
Supination (Fencing p13)	51
Pronation (Fencing p29)	51
On Guard (Fencing p17)	52
Lunge (Fencing p20)	52
Parry of Quarte (Fencing p40)	52

Riposte from parry of quarte (Fencing p89)   53
A Plunger (Badminton p161)   57
Backing Up (Badminton p176)   58
The Experienced Mountaineer (Sketchbook)   59
The Willink Family in 1890 (Photograph - F)   60
Initial S – Incidence and reflection (Badminton p149)   61
Highwoods (Photograph – MS)   62
In the Chimney (Snap Frontispiece)   64
Snap's Sacrifice (Snap facing p278)   65
Mr. Thomas Bland Garland (Sketchbook)   69
Clinton Thomas Dent (Sketchbook)   70
Serve Him Right (Badminton facing p104)   72
Crack Climbers (Badminton p232)   73
Henry sketching (Photograph - F)   74
Revised edition H. G. Willink (Poor Law, Photograph -   79
MS)
Sir George Nicholls (Poor Law, Frontispiece)   80
Initial F – Hamlet iii 1, 81 (Badminton p39)   81
Hillfields (Photograph – F)   88
Initial B (Badminton p307)   89
Three Little Fairies (Photograph - F)   100
The Willink Family c1900 (Photograph - F)   103
Interior of Hillfields (Photograph - F)   104
Hillfields 1912   105
Old Berkshire Shield (several places on internet)   106
Initial O – Over it goes! (Badminton p215)   107
Silver Wedding Bronze Plaque (Photograph - F)   113
George skiing (Sketchbook)   114
Arrival in New York (Sketchbook)   115
Near Hyères, France (Sketchbook)   119
Marriage of Katie and Ned (Photograph - F)   120
Initial M – Topographers (Badminton p263)   121
Henry and Mary on their motor tour (Photograph - F) x2   123
Noel and Ba (Photograph - F)   125
Capt. F. A. Willink, 1915 (Photograph - F)   129
Capt. G. O. W. Willink, 1917 (Photograph - F)   129
Henry, Francis, George and Mary, 1917 (Photograph - F)   131
Memorial Tablet – Mary Grace Willink (Photograph –   133
MS)

Memorial Tablet – George O. W. Willink (Photograph – MS)   134

Ba and Honor (Photograph - F)   136

Mary's gravestone, 1919 (Photograph - F)   137

Capt. G. O. W. Willink M.C. gravestone (Photograph - F)   137

Burghfield War Cross Dedication (Photograph - F)   139

Henry in July 1921 (Photograph - F)   140

Initial C – A mountain arab (Badminton p206)   141

Burneside weathervane (Photograph - F)   144

Hillfields weathervane at The Willink School (Photograph – MS)   145

Rector and Churchwardens (Photograph - F)   147

Highfield (Sketchbook)   149

Dunham Oaks (Sketchbook)   150

Mary & Henry's gravestone (Photograph – MS)   154

Memorial Tablet – Henry George Willink (Photograph – MS)   155

Hillfields by John Piper (Painting in the family's possession and used with permission)   156

Leonard and Hester Dent (Photographs – F)

Initial T – A Professor on a T-table (Badminton p186)   157

Initial I – An I Glass (Badminton p348)   159

Index

Abery, Mr. 96
Acorns 3, 4
Alderman ix, 107, 110, 118, 125
Almer, Ulrich 51
Alpine Club 19, 43, 45, 55, 102, 121
Alpine Distress Signal Scheme 97
Alpine Journal 43, 45, 117
Alps 19, 21, 22, 27, 31, 43, 55, 69, 92, 93, 96, 102, 112, 148
Allotments & Small Holdings Committee 111
Amsterdam 5
Andermatt 22
Antique Collector 157
Antwerp 26
Argentière 112
Armistice 135
Ashwicke Hall 22
Assessment & County Boundaries Committee 111
Assize Courts 77, 118
Athenaeum Club 152
Attendance medal 108, 109
Austria/Austrian 25, 26
Avonmouth 115
Bache de Sagte, Henry Valentine 40
Badminton Library 69, 71, 92, 121
Badminton Magazine 97
Badminton Mountaineering book 69-71, 76, 121
Bamberg 25
Barings 7
Barn Hey 8, 11, 12
Barningham, William 61, 62
Barranva pass 25
Basle 21

Bath (city of) 22
Belgium/Belgian 11, 124, 141
Bell Ringing Society 115
Bellagio 119
Bennet, T. J. 122
Bennet's Hill 97
Benyon, Mr. J. Herbert 73, 100, 109, 110, 138
Bergen 35
Berkshire 56, 62, 77, 78, 81, 106-109, 138, 142, 153, 154
Berkshire Chronicle 111
Berkshire Club 153
Berkshire National Relief Fund Committee 126
Berkshire County Council ix, 108-112, 116, 118, 125, 142, 148
Berkshire County Council Technical Education Committee 99
Berkshire Education Committee ix, 108-110, 116, 125, 142, 148, 151-153
Berkshire National Reserve 124
Berkshire Quarter Sessions of the Peace 77
Berkshire Record Office 89
Berkshire shield 106,109
Berkshire War Agriculture Committee 126
Bermuda 21
Berne 22
Bernese Oberland/Alps 22, 31
Bernina Pass 25
Bethune 135
Betjeman, John 157
Big Game Shooting 92
Birmingham iv, 8, 9, 10, 38, 39, 122

Birmingham Canal Navigations Company 9, 38-40, 47, 92, 116
Blake, Mr. 99
Bland, Emily (*née* Cherry) 68
Bland, Horatio 67, 68, 89
Bland Garland, Thomas 67-69, 74, 75, 84, 89, 91
Blands Court 107
Blomfield, Sir Reginald R.A. 139
Boldrewood ix
Bolivia 67
Bonn 21
Boulogne 19
Bournemouth 130
Bowcher, Frank 108
Bowdon 150
Bradfield District Tribunal 126
Bradfield Guardians of the Poor 9, 67, 74, 83-87, 92, 96, 111, 112, 126, 127
Bradfield Rural District Council (see also Sanitary Authority of Bradfield Union) 67, 100, 116, 125-127
Bradfield Rural District Council School Attendance Sub-committee 108
Bradfield Workhouse 78, 83
Breithorn 31
Breukelen 19, 140, 141
Brévent 19
Brickyard Cover 97
Bridge (cards) 76
Britain/Great Britain/British 10, 26, 53, 71, 92, 121, 130
Brock, Isabel 66
Brock, Rev. Thomas 66
Brown, Edward F.L.S. 99
Brown, Georgina (Na) 32, 124, 146
Brussels 6, 21, 26
Bryant, Dr. Walter 61
Buckingham Palace 130

Buckinghamshire 42, 44, 132
Bucks Herald 42
Buildings & Repair Section 108
Bungalow, Hillfields 68
Burghfield ix, 3, 4, 56, 62, 63, 66, 68, 75, 82, 86, 89, 93-99, 101, 103, 107, 110, 111, 115, 116, 121, 124, 128, 130, 133-135, 137-139, 142, 143, 146-148, 152, 155
Burghfield and Sulhamstead Horticultural Show/Society 71, 94, 116
Burghfield Brass Band 138
Burghfield Common 68, 122, 124, 138, 145
Burghfield Cricket Club 95, 116
Burghfield Hill 61, 75, 89
Burghfield Infant School 73
Burghfield Lodge of Oddfellows – see Oddfellows ("Loyal Star of the West" Lodge)
Burghfield National Schools (also Burghfield Old School) 98, 107, 124, 142
Burghfield New Schools 137, 143
Burghfield Parish Council 96, 122, 137
Burghfield Parish Magazine 93, 94, 99, 100, 105, 132, 135, 142, 148
Burghfield Secondary Modern School ix
Burghfield Schools Managers 116, 142
Burghfield United Charities 142
Burn, William 61
Burneside 143, 144
Burnett, Colin 145
Buttermere 143
Bye-Laws and School Attendance Section 108
Bye-Laws committee 96

Cader Idris 28, 59
Calais 17, 26
Calkin, Lance (painter) xii
Callas, Messers. 99
Callipers Hall 15-17, 56 – also see Winton House
Canadian 21
Canning, Capt. 50
Caucasus 71
Caves, H. 43
Ceylon 9, 118
Chamonix 19, 22, 112
Chance, Ernest 111
Chancery Bar 31
Charity Organization Review 81
Charity Organization Society (also see Reading Charity Organization Society) 81, 82, 84
Cherry, Rev. Henry Curtis 68
Cherry, Emily – see Bland, Emily
Cheshire 5, 147, 150
Chignell, Alma Marion – see Willink, Marion
Chignell, Rev. Hendrick 152
Chignell, Margaret 148
Chile 67, 68
China/Chinese 102, 104
Chipperfield Common 15, 17
Christian, Prince of Schleswig-Holstein 98
Christiana 21
Churchwarden 9, 115, 116, 142, 147
Clark, Col. 50 (possibly the same person as Clark, Gerard Collingwood)
Clark, Gerard Collingwood 35, 136, 141
Clark, Harriet Delamain (*née* Ouvry) (Known as Harry) iv, 26, 38, 42, 43, 76, 101, 117, 136, 141
Clark, Hester – see Dent, Hester

Clark, Maisie (actual name Aimée) 100, 101, 117
Claydon, Mr. 99
Clay Hill 97
Clifford's Inn Hall 97
Clifton & Kersley Colliery 121
Climbs in the New Zealand Alps 97
Clinton, Rev. William Osbert 56
Cobham, Captain A. W. 77, 118
Codrington, Captain 45
Col de la Seigne 19
Colma Pass 25
Cologne 25
Como 25, 118
Coniston Old Man 150
Conservative and Unionist 101
Cooper, Frederick E. 66
Copenhagen 21
Coquimbo Railway Company 68
Cornwall 8, 17, 122
Cory, William – see Johnson, William
County Council' Association 116
Courmayeur 19
Covent Garden 94
Cradley 51
Crete 16
Cricket 63, 76, 94, 95, 116, 117, 138
Cuillin Hills 27
Culverlands 61, 93, 96, 98
Daisy (cow) 146
Daisy (donkey) 100
Danube 26
Davies, Duncan 159
Davies Janet 159
Davies, Mr. 84
Dent, Anita 141
Dent, Celia 141, 148, 159
Dent, Clinton Thomas 45, 69-71, 75, 76, 97, 117, 118
Dent, Edward 76

Dent, Gerard 141, 145, 159
Dent, Hester (*née* Clark) 76, 100, 101, 117, 141, 154, 156, 157, 159
Dent, Major Leonard M. E., DSO ix, 76, 101, 141, 156, 157
Dent, Rosalind 141, 148
Dent, Theresa 141
Devil's Own – see Inns of Court Volunteers
Dewe, James 68
Dictionary of National Biography 151
Dijon 22
Dingwall 26
Diphtheria 69
Dobson, Austin 46
Dordrecht 25
Dormer, Mr. 96
Dover 17, 26
Dragon 22, 23
Dunham Oaks 150
Dunn, H. A. Colmore 51, 53
Dutch Home Labour Colonies, The 82
East India Company 9
Education Act (1870) 94
Education Act (1902) 108
Edward VII 104
Eggishorn 22
Elementary Education sub-committee 108
Elm 22
Englefield 73
Eton College 14, 17, 18, 45, 56, 103, 117, 155
Eton "fives" 18
Evans, Arthur 16
Evans, Sam 18
Eversley 103
Fareham 17
Farndon 9, 67
Farrell, Lieut. Col. 50

Fawcett, Preston & Co. – see Phoenix Iron Foundry
Fencing 18, 19, 45, 51, 53, 54
Fiat Tipo Zero Torpedo 123
Finance Committee 96, 116
Finsteraahorn 31
Finstermünz 25
Fireworks 138
Fitzgerald, E. A. 97
Flanders 128
Fleet Street 97
Flims 22
Fobello 25
Fodderty Lodge 26
Fontainebleau 22
Food Economy Sub-committee 127
Football 18, 71, 95
France/French 6, 15, 18, 19, 53, 94, 112, 118, 119, 128, 130, 133-135, 137, 141
Frankfurt 21, 25
Franklin, Benjamin 94
Franklin Institute 94, 95
Furka 22
Gabelhorn 50
Galenstock 31
Garland, Henry 74
Garland, Thomas Bland – see Bland Garland, Thomas
Gemmi Pass 22
Geological Survey 99
George III 30
George V 130
George, Rev. W. H. 122, 147
Germany/German 6, 19, 21, 130
Gibraltar 118
Gladstone, Mr. W. E. 86, 101
Glarus 21
Glen, Alexander 48, 49
Gloucestershire 122
Golf 76
Grazeley 122

Guardians of the Poor of
  Bradfield Union 9
Gloucester & Berkeley Canal 9,
  38
Graphic, The 50
Grazebrook, Owen F. 40
Great Sugar Loaf Hill 102
Green Gable 146
Grey, E. C. 94
Guide Dogs for The Blind
  Association 155, 156
Gunterstein Castle 19, 20
Greenaway, Kate 30
Grindelwald 22, 23
Guernsey 66
Gummers How 26
Hale, Col. Lonsdale 50
Hall, Col. Julian H. 50
Hancock, Mary 159
Handbells 99
Harding, John 96
Harington, Alice 66
Harington, Florence 66
Harington, Rev. Dallas Oldfield
  66, 98
Harrow 16
Hasheen, Battle of 49
Haslam & Son, Messrs. 75
Hawley, Gen. 68
Hebuterne 135
Heidelberg 21
Helvellyn 27, 92
Higgs & Son, Burghfield 139
High Crag 143
High Stile 143
High Street (Cumbria) 27
Highfield, Worsley 148, 149, 157
Highway committee 96
Highwoods 61-63, 67, 68, 71, 76,
  78, 91, 93, 94, 117, 146
Hillfields 67, 68, 75, 77, 78, 88-
  91, 94, 95-97, 101, 103-105,
  107, 110, 114, 116, 117, 121,
122, 124, 126, 130, 136, 138,
  145, 146, 152, 155-157, 159
Hillfields Farm 91
Hodgson, surgeon 1
Holland 8, 25, 82, 148 – also see
  Netherlands
Hollybush Lane 145
Huyton 1, 46, 47
Hyde Park Street 10, 12, 13, 15,
  29, 38, 42, 46, 47
Hyères 118, 119
Ilanz 22
Indoor relief 84, 85, 112
Infant School – see Burghfield
  Infant School
Ingleside 141
Inner Temple 35, 117
Inns of Court School of Arms 51
Inns of Court Volunteers 30, 45,
  48-51, 53, 54, 124, 128
Interlaken 22
Ireland 10, 102, 118
Irish Church Mission Society 66
Italy/Italian 6, 7, 19, 25, 43, 93,
  118, 122
Jackson, Noel x
Jamaica 115
Jebb, George Robert 40, 92
Jenkins & Son, Torquay 139
Jersey cows 145, 146
Jerusalem 68
Johns, Rev. Charles Alexander
  15, 16
Johnson, Mrs. 143
Johnson, William 17
Jubilee Room 98, 99, 124
Justice of the Peace/ J.P. 77, 78,
  111, 116, 130
Kandersteg 22
Kendal 144
Kings Hill 99
Kingston, Jamaica 115
Kirton's farm 107

195

Knossos 16
Lake District/Lakeland 26, 27, 31, 35, 50, 92, 143, 146, 150, 159
Lakeland Memories 27, 35
Lamotte-en-Santerre 133, 137
Langdale Pike 27
Lapland 35
Latham, Alfred 12
Latham, Anne – see Willink, Anne
Latham, Charles 5
Laurent family 124
Lauterbrunnen 22
Law Times 31
Leela 146
Leghorn, Italy 7
Leighton Buzzard 43, 54, 55, 85
Leighton Buzzard Observer and Linslade Gazette 54
Le Presse 25
Leukerbad 22
Liberal Unionist 101, 102
Libraries 142, 143
Lincoln's Inn 27, 30, 31, 45, 94
Linnean Society 16
Linz 26
Liverpool 1, 5, 6-8, 10-12, 15, 29, 46, 47, 98, 118
Lloyd, A. T. 153
Lo Besso 112
Local Government Bill (1893) 86
Local Government Act (1894) 86, 96, 101
Loch, Sir Charles 81
Lockinge House 97
London 1, 5, 6, 8, 10, 12, 15, 21, 22, 27, 29, 38, 39, 43, 45, 56, 76, 78, 81, 87, 94, 95, 117, 118, 123, 135, 146, 152, 157
London clay 99
London County Council 123
London Daily News 87

London Gazette 135
Longman's Magazine 48
Lord Lieutenant of Berkshire 138, 154
Lousley, Job 137, 143, 147
Louvain 124
Low Borrow Bridge 143
Luton Times and Advertiser 43
Lyon, Alfred Charles 40
Mackay, Mr. T. 87
Macugnaga 22
Magazine of Arts, The 45
Malmo 21
Maltby, Brough 9, 67
Maltby, Brough (Archdeacon) 67
Maltby, Harriet – see Nicholls, Harriet
Maltby, Mary 9
Manchester 93, 121, 122, 136, 141, 148, 158
Manchester Collieries Ltd 148
Map-flapping 48,49
Mappin & Webb 109
Marseilles 118
Marshfield 22
Martigny 19
Martinsbruck 25
Martins-Loch 22
Matterhorn 31, 41
Mattingley, Francis 96
Mawson, Rev. Hector 74
Mayne, L. 69
Mediterranean 21, 118
Melbourne, Lord 9
Milan 25
Millwall Docks 36
Möerdyke 25, 26
Mönch 31
Monck, John Bligh 77
Moncrieff, Col. G. H. 50
Mont Blanc 22, 55
Monte Moro Pass 22
Morbegno 25

Morning Post 16
Mosdell, C. 92
Mount, Mr. William Arthur 101, 102
Mount, Mr. W. G. 101
Mrs. Bland's School 107, 142
Mrs. Bland's Infant School ix
Munich 25
Mürren 22
Myers, Bland & Co. 67
Neobard, H. J. C. 109
Netherlands 3, 11, 19, 25, 81, 82, 140, 153
Neuchâtel 22
New York 115
Newbury Art Society 97
Newfoundland 67
Nicholls, Georgiana E. (Aunt Georgie) 26, 29, 42, 46, 47
Nicholls, Charlotte – see Wingfield, Charlotte
Nicholls, George (Sir) 38, 43
  Bank of England, Birmingham, manager 9
  Birmingham Canal Navigations Company 9, 38, 39
  biography by HGW 87, 151
  birth 8
  Captain 9
  death 29
  death of two daughters 10
  History of the English Poor Law 79, 81, 87, 151
  Honours – CB & KCB 10
  In Ireland 10
  life at sea 8, 9
  memorial plaque 67
  Poor Law 9, 10
  Poor Law Board Secretary 10, 80
  Poor Law Commissioner 10, 80, 81
  ships served on 9

Southwell 9, 67
Nicholls, Harriet (*née* Maltby) 9, 38, 43
  death 29
  death of two daughters 10
  memorial plaque 67
  Southwell 9, 67
Nicholls, Jane – see Ouvry, Jane
Nordfjord 37
Northenden 147, 148
Norway 31, 35, 37
Nottinghamshire 67
Nuremberg 25
Oberalpstock 31
Oddfellows ("Loyal Star of the West" Lodge, Burghfield) 93, 101, 116, 151
Orred, Annie 38
Orred, Catharina Mary (*née* Willink) 22
Orred, Edith 38
Orred, Frances (*née* Hilton) 22
Orred, John 22
Orred, Katie 38
Orred, Randal 38
Orred, Woodville 38
Orta, Lake 25
Oslo 35 – also see Christiana
Ouvry, Aimee 43
Ouvry coat of arms/shield 4
Ouvry, Colonel C.B. 42
Ouvry, Constance 43
Ouvry, Ernest Carrington 69, 104
Ouvry, Ethel 43
Ouvry, Francisca 43
Ouvry, Harriet Delamain – see Clark, Harriet Delamain
Ouvry, Jane (*née* Nicholls) 43, 44
Ouvry, Rev. John Delahaize 122, 153
Ouvry, Mary Grace – see Willink, Mary Grace

197

Ouvry, Peter T. (Rev.) 42-44, 47, 50
Outdoor relief 9, 84-86, 112
Oxford, Lord Bishop of 75, 103
Oxford Diocese 132
Oxford University 16, 27, 30, 66, 112
  Brasenose College 18, 117, 124
  Corpus Christi College 117
Pacific 17
Paddington 11, 13, 29, 46, 47, 50, 82, 94
Padworth 56
Pall Mall Gazette 71
Palladium Life Assurance Society 6
Paris 18, 19, 22
Parochial Church Council 142, 148
Patterdale 92
Peace Celebration 138
Pell, Albert 86
Pembroke (Pem) 145, 155
Perrier, Marie 66
Phillips, Charles 43
Phillipps-Wolley, Clive 62, 92
Phoenix Iron Foundry 7, 8, 11
Piedmont 22
Pilkington, Catharine Dorothy (*née* Willink) (Katie) 31, 47, 60, 100, 101, 105, 107, 118-121, 124, 126, 136, 141, 147, 150, 153
  1891 census 63
  1911 census 117
  baptism 47
  birth 47
  children – see entries on
    Pilkington, Noel Mary
    Pilkington, Honor Brocklehurst
  confirmation 103
  marriage 121

Pilkington, Charles 121
Pilkington, Charles George Willink 141, 146, 159
Pilkington, Denis 147
Pilkington, D. T. 43
Pilkington, Edward Fielden (Ned) 120, 121, 147, 150, 153
Pilkington, Edward Michael (known as Michael) 141, 148
Pilkington, Honor Brocklehurst 126, 136, 141, 148
Pilkington, Noel Mary 124, 136, 141, 148, 160
Pilkington Tiles 121
Pillar Rock 31, 34, 35
Pingewood School 107
Piper, John 156, 157
Pirno 25
Plug Street 135
Pointe de Galle 9
Police Special Reserve 126
Pontresina 25
Poor Law Amendment Act 10
Poor Law conferences 67
Povey, Mr. 84
Port St. Vincent 118
Portman Club 95
Poynton, Sir Edward 30
Princes Park 1, 3, 11
Princess (horse) 100
Princess of Orange 6, 7
Progressive Party 96
Prospect Park 98
Public Health Committee 111
Punch 31
Pyrenees 27, 31
Quarles van Ufford, Albertine (*née* Willink van Collen) 19, 141
Quarles van Ufford, Louis 19, 141
Queenie (cow) 146
Reading 56, 75, 89, 93, 97, 99, 110, 112, 152

Reading Assize Courts 77, 118
Reading Charity Organization
  Society 84, 116
Reading County Bench 77
Reading Mercury 74, 77, 84, 95,
  104, 109, 128, 130, 134
Reading Savings Bank 76, 77,
  101, 116
Reading University (also
  University College) 112, 116,
  148, 156
Recreation Ground 122, 138
Red Pike 143
Rhine 21
Rhone Glacier 22
Ricardo, Col. G. C. 118
Richmond, Thomas (painter) 2
Rickmansworth 15
Ridge, Major 50
Roby 8, 11, 47
Roche, M. 15
Romansch 22
Rome 103
Rosendaal 26
Rosenlaui 22
Rothschild, Leopold de 42
Rotterdam 25
Rowlandson, Thomas 157
Royal Academy Schools 18
Royal Berks Seed Establishment
  Cricket Club 95
Royal Berkshire Friendly Society
  101, 116
Royal Berkshire Hospital 98
Royal Berkshire Regiment 124,
  128, 138
Royal College of Surgeons 76
Royal Counties' Agricultural
  Show 97
Royal Military Tournament 45
Royal United Service Institution
  48
Royal Victoria Hall, London 56

Royal Watercolour Society 18, 30
Russia 35
Saas 22
Salisbury Plain 135
Samaden 25
Sanitary Authority of Bradfield
  Union (see also Bradfield Rural
  District Council) 67-69, 74, 83,
  84, 86, 92, 96, 126
Santiago 68
Sardinia Street Mission 94
Scale Force 143
Scarborough 118
Scarlet fever 1, 2
Schilthorn 22
School Management Section/Sub-
  committee 108, 150
Scilly Isles 17
Scotland/Scottish 26, 118
Scots Magazine, The 63
Sca(w)fell Pike 27
Sedburgh 143
Shaw, A. P. 151
Shepherd, Rev. Alfred J. P. 111,
  127
Skalstugan 37
Skiddaw 27
Skye 27
Slade School of Art 30
Smith, Lieut. G. R. 45
*Snap – A Legend of the Lone
  Mountain* 62, 63-65, 92
Snowdon 150
Snowdonia 26
Somme 134, 141
Sondrio 25
South Africa 102
South America 67, 68
South Berks Hunt 97
Southwell 9, 67
Spey 25, 26
Spiers, Col. 50
Sri Lanka – see Ceylon

Stavanger 35
Sterling, Col. 50
Stockholm 21, 35, 36
Strasbourg 19
St. George's Hospital Medical School 76
St. John the Baptist's Church, Princes Park 2
St. John's Church, Paddington 11, 47, 50
St. Laurence's Church, Reading 112
St. Mary's Church, Acton 47
St. Mary's Church, Burghfield 3, 4, 62, 66, 68, 74, 103, 115, 116, 121, 124, 130, 133, 134, 136-138, 142, 147, 148, 152, 153, 155
St. Michael's Church, Huyton 1, 46
St. Neot's School 103
St. Peter Port, Guernsey 66
St. Petersburg 35
St. Peter's Church, Farndon 67
St. Wilfred's Church, Northenden 147
Steeds, Mjr. John 159
Sulhamstead 66, 71, 94, 97
Summers, Cathy v, 159
Sweden 31, 35-37
Switzerland/Swiss 19, 25, 27, 30, 31, 43, 55, 66, 69, 70, 102, 112, 145
Tactical and War Game Society (Home District) 50
Tarasp 25
Tattam, Alice L. 66
Taylor, Alice 66
Taylor, James 61
Telford, June 66
Telford, Thomas 9
Theale 95, 99, 107
Théodule Pass 19

Thursby, Arthur H. 96, 115
Thursby, Rev. Harvey W. G. 152
Tindall, John 54, 55
Tindall, Robert 55
Titlis 31
Tower, Brownlow 17
Toxteth Park 6, 8
Trash Green 99
Treherne, Jane 15
Tresco 17
Trinity 67
Trondheim 35
Tryfaen 31
Typhoid fever 69
Ufton Wood 97
Ullswater 92
United States of America /American 5, 21, 115
University College – see Reading University
Urlwin, J. 95
Valparaiso 67
Van Collen, Johanna 19
Varallo 25
Venice 148
Victoria, Princess 98
Victoria, Queen 10, 98, 104
Vidal, Rev. F and House at Eton 17
Viesch 22
Villach 26
Viller-Bretonneux Cemetery 134
Visp 22
Walker, J. W. 151
Wantage, Lady 97
Wantage, Lord 97
War Memorial Cross 138, 139, 152
Warrington, Emma M. 66
Warrington, Thomas Rolls 66
Wastwater 27
Watford 15, 16
Weathervane 144, 145

Weekly Reporter 31
Wellington Barracks 49
Westminster Town Hall 50
Weston-super-Mare 135
Wetterhorn 22, 31
Whitby 118
Wiesbaden 25
Wilderwurm 22, 23
Williamson, Joseph 5
Willink, Alfred Henry 3, 144
Willink, Anne (*née* Latham) –
  also known as Grandmamma
  Willink 3, 11, 29
  death 29
  marriage to Daniel Willink 5
Willink, Arthur 38
Willink, Catharine Dorothy
  (Katie) – see Pilkington,
  Catharine Dorothy
Willink, Catharine Harriet (*née*
  Nicholls) 2, 43, 44
  birth 8
  burial 1, 46
  children – see entries on:
    Willink, Harriet
    Willink, William Nicholls
    Willink, Henry George
  death 1, 11
  marriage to William Williamson
  Willink 11
Willink, Cecilia Jane Francis de
  Chantal (*née* Wingfield) (Lily)
  38, 43
  child – see Willink, Thomas
  Wingfield
  death 51
  marriage 38
Willink coat of arms/shield x, 3,
  4
Willink family motto ix, x, 4, 159
Willink, Daniel 3, 4
  bankruptcy 5, 6
  birth 5

commission merchant 6
Consul for the Kingdom of the
  Netherlands 5
death 29
Knight of the Order of the
  Netherland Lion 8, 10
marriage to Anne Latham 5
merchant 5
Willink, Francis Arthur ix, 112,
  131, 136, 141, 148, 149
  1891 census 66
  1911 census 117
  baptism 62
  birth 62
  Birmingham Canal Navigations
  40
  holiday in Jamaica and New
  York 115
  inheritance 155
  invalided from army 128, 135
  marriage 147
  Royal Berkshire Regiment 124,
  129, 135
  sale of Hillfields 157
  school 103
  Silver War Badge Roll 135
  Uncle Fa 124
  university 117, 124
  war record 127, 128, 135
Willink, George Ouvry William
  102, 112, 114, 131, 137, 139,
  141
  1891 census 66
  1911 census 117
  baptism 50
  birth 50
  burial 134
  Inns of Court Volunteers 124,
  128
  killed in action 133
  memorial tablet 3, 134
  Mentioned in Despatches 128
  Military Cross 128

missing in action 133
Royal Berkshire Regiment 128-
    130
schools 103
university 117
Willink, Harriet 1, 11, 46
Willink, Henry George (Ba)
  1 (formerly 17) Hyde Park St.
    47
  8 New Court, Lincoln's Inn 45
  29 Albion Street 46, 47
  1891 census 63, 65
  1911 census 117
  Alderman ix, 118
  Alpine Club 43, 45, 55, 102
  appendicitis 75, 76, 117
  Army signalling exam 49
  Ba 6, 124, 125, 136, 146, 160
  Badminton Mountaineering
    book 69-71
  baptism 3
  barrister 27
  Berkshire County Council 110
  Berkshire shield 106, 109
  Birmingham Canal Navigations
    39, 40, 47, 92, 116
  biography of his father 150, 151
  biography of his grandfather 87,
    151
  birth 1, 11
  Bradfield Guardian of the Poor
    9, 67, 83-87, 92, 96, 111, 112,
    126, 127
  burial 153
  called to the Bar 31
  Callipers 15-17, 56
  children – see entries for
    Willink, John Ouvry
    Willink, Catharine Dorothy
    Willink, George Ouvry
      William
    Willink, Francis Arthur
  churchwarden 115, 116, 142,
    147
  cricket 94, 95, 116
  death x, 151, 152
  degree 27
  drawing 18 – also see sketching
  Dutch family, 19, 21, 25, 141
  editing Parish Magazine 128,
    142
  Education Committee, Berkshire
    County Council ix, 108-110,
    116, 125, 142, 148, 151-153
  estate 153
  Eton 17, 18, 117
  father's death 46
  fencing 18, 19, 45, 51, 53, 54
  football 18
  French 15, 18
  funeral 152, 153
  governess 15
  Guardian of the Poor 9
  Highwoods – moving in 62
  Hillfields purchase 75, 89-91
  History of the English Poor Law
    79, 81, 87, 151
  holiday in Jamaica and New
    York 115
  illness 75, 126, 142, 150, 151
  illustrations 4, 31, 45, 46, 50, 51,
    62, 63, 69, 70, 71, 93, 96, 97
  inheritance 47
  Inns of Court Volunteers 30, 45,
    48-51, 53, 54
  journalism 31
  Jubilee Room 98, 99, 124
  Justice of the Peace 77, 78, 111,
    116, 130
  Kings Hill well 99
  Lake District 26, 27, 31, 35, 50,
    92, 143, 146, 150
  lectures on mountaineering 19,
    54-56
  map-flapping 48
  marriage 42

memorial tablet 4, 155
motor tour 122, 123
mountaineering 19, 21, 22, 25,
  27, 31, 35, 50, 102, 112
National Reserve 124
pauperism – views 82-85
politics 101
Poor Law conferences 67, 82, 86
Paddington Guardian of the
  Poor 82
Reading University Council
  Vice President 112, 148
rowing 18
school named in his honour ix
sketch book 35
sketching 22, 43, 48, 50, 54, 71,
  74, 112, 150
Slade School of Art 30
Snowdonia 26
Winton House 17
Willink Hof 19
Willink, Jan Abraham (older) 5
Willink, Jan Abraham (younger)
  47
Willink, John Ouvry 47, 48
Willink, Rev. Canon John
  Wakefield 122
Willink, Marion (née Chignell)
  147, 149
Willink, Mary Grace (née Ouvry)
  26, 38, 43, 44, 46, 47, 50, 60,
  66, 75, 76, 97, 98, 103, 104,
  107, 112, 118, 122, 123, 124,
  126-128, 131-133, 136, 137,
  146, 153, 154
  1891 census 63
  1911 census 117
  children – see entries for
    Willink, John Ouvry
    Willink, Catharine Dorothy
    Willink, George Ouvry
     William
    Willink, Francis Arthur

  death 130
  funeral 130
  grave 137
  marriage 42
  memorial tablet 132, 133
  Mothers' meeting 66
  Parish Room choir 66
Willink School, The iv, vi, ix, x,
  4, 76, 122, 145
Willink, Thomas Wingfield 47,
  51, 67
Willink van Collen, Daniel 19
Willink, Wilhem 5, 7, 8
Willink, William Edward 98
Willink, William Nicholls (Willy)
  42-44
  birth 11
  child – see Willink, Thomas
    Wingfield
  climbing 26-28, 31, 35
  death 51, 67
  death of wife 51
  description by HGW 21
  Eclipse, HMS 21, 26
  inheritance 47
  Law career 35
  leaving Navy 26
  marriage 38
  memorial plaque 67
  Naval Cadet 17
  Pallas, HMS 21
  Scandinavia 35
  school 15, 17
  Sutlej, HMS 17, 21
  wife's death 51
Willink, William Williamson xii,
  1, 3, 29, 42, 44
  baptism 5
  Birmingham Canal Navigations
    39
  biography by HGW 150, 151
  birth 5
  career 6-8

children – see entries on:
  Willink, Harriet
  Willink, William Nicholls
  Willink, Henry George
death 46
education 5, 6
funeral 46
ill abroad 25, 26
Italian business 7
languages spoken 6
marriage to Catharine Nicholls 11
mountaineering 21, 22, 25
Phoenix Iron Foundry 7, 8, 11
Princess of Orange's jewels 6, 7
Secretary to Public Works Loan Commissioners 12
stroke 46
Vice Consul for the Netherlands 8
will 46
Willink, Willy (cousin) 38
Wimbledon Common 49
Winchester 17

Windermere 26, 50
Windmill Hill 135
Wing 42, 44, 132
Wingfield, Cecilia Jane Francis de Chantal – see Willink, Cecilia Jane Francis de Chantal
Wingfield, Charlotte (née Nicholls) 38, 43
Wingfield, Edmund (Eddy) 35, 38
Wingfield, Gertrude 38
Wingfield, Sophie 38
Wingfield, William (Rev) 38, 43
Winterswyk 19
Winton House 17
Women's Institute 146
Workhouse 78, 82-85
Working Men's Club 98, 99
Worsley 148, 157
Wray Cottage 50
Young, Geoffrey Winthrop 45
Ypres 141
Zermatt 19, 50
Zurich 19

Printed in Great Britain
by Amazon

46876028R00126